A HALF–DAY'S RIDE

OR

ESTATES IN CORSICA

by *Padraic* *Colum*

A HALF-DAY'S RIDE

RIDE

or

ESTATES IN CORSICA

by

Padraic Colum

New York

THE MACMILLAN COMPANY

1932

PRINTED IN THE UNITED STATES OF AMERICA
NORWOOD PRESS LINOTYPE, INC.
NORWOOD, MASS., U.S.A.

TO MY FRIENDS
AGNES AND JOHN CAVANAGH

For permission to include in this volume certain essays, the author returns thanks to the editors of the following publications: Everyman, the Commonweal (three essays), the New Republic (two), the Nation (five), the Spectator, the Dial (four), the Saturday Review of Literature, the Bookman (New York), the New Statesman, the Catholic World, the Dublin Magazine, the Theatre Arts Magazine.

CONTENTS

[ix]

A HALF–DAY'S RIDE

OR

ESTATES IN CORSICA

A DAY'S RIDE

Last night at the circus I found myself thinking of Charles Lever's seldom-read novel, "A Day's Ride, a Life's Romance." The impetus had gone out of the proceedings, the band blared no more, the crack of the ring-master's whip no longer resounded; the spangled lady, whose feats of horsewomanship were below what we had expected, sat on her steed, while the ring-master and the clown rubbed up a dialogue that was barely entertaining. Why did these slack moments remind me of the life's romance of Algernon Sydney Potts? Because it would be in such subdued vagabondage that Lever's hero would find himself. Indeed, that clown in ultra-evening dress, with chalk-covered countenance, might be Potts himself at the moment of a new disillusionment.

There is a circus horse in "A Day's Ride," and there are circus people too—old Vaterchen and little Tinte-fleck or Catinka. Yet it is not only because of these performers that the story reminds me of the circus and the circus reminds me of the story. If he had started off on any other horse—ay, if he had never fallen in with old Vaterchen and little Catinka, Algernon Sydney Potts

would have known the canvas and the ring. He tries
to assure us that he settled down in Wales, and lived
blamelessly ever afterwards with Kate Herbert or Mary
Crofton, or whoever was the paragon who held his heart.
But I believe that the end pages in "A Day's Ride" are
Potts' last pretence. His ghost still crosses the space
that is shadowy in the sunlight and that flares in the
naphtha light. And does that not prove that in the
flesh Potts knew the scene? Consider the soliloquy in
the arbour when he took off his hat and bowed respect-
fully to the members of an imaginary court:

"My name," said I, in a clear and respectful voice, "is Algernon Sydney Potts. If I be pushed to the avowal, I am sorry
it *is* Potts! Algernon Sydney do a deal, but they can't do everything—not to say that captious folk see a certain bathos in the
collocation with my surname. Can a man hope to make such
a name illustrious? Can he aspire to the notion of a time when
people will allude to the great Potts, the celebrated Potts, the im-
mortal Potts?" I grew very red, I felt my cheek on fire as I uttered this, and I suddenly bethought me of Mr. Pitt, and I said
aloud, "And if Pitt, why not Potts?" That was a most healing
reflection. I revelled in it for a long time. "How true it is,"
I continued, "that the halo of greatness illumines all within its
circle, and the man is merged in the grandeur of his achieve-
ments. The men who start in life with high-sounding designa-
tions have but to fill a foregone pledge—to pay the bill that
Fortune has endorsed. Not so was our case, Pitt. To us is it
to lay every foundation-stone of our future greatness. There
was nothing in *your* surname to foretell you would be Minister
of State at one and thirty—there is no letter of *mine* to indicate
what I shall be. But what is it that I am to be? Is it Poet,
Philosopher, Politician, Soldier or Discoverer? Am I to be

A Day's Ride

great in Art or illustrious in Letters? Is there to be an ice tract in Behring's Straits called Potts' Point, or a planet styled Pottsium Sidus? And when centuries have rolled over, will historians have their difficulty about the first Potts, and what his opinions were on this subject or that?"

Surely these words sealed Algernon Sydney of the tribe of whoever the patriarch is of those who display themselves in tents.

There was something quite moderate in the way Potts entered into his life's romance. He knew that a horse was requisite, but he decided not to buy but to hire one. He thought he would take his mount from day to day, so that if any change of mind or purpose supervened he should not be in any embarrassment. In Dycer's Yard he found a beast to his liking.

I liked the creature's eye. It was soft, mild and contemplative; and although not remarkable for brilliancy, possessed a subdued lustre that promised well for temper and disposition. "Ten shillings a day—make it three half-crowns by the week, sir. You'll never hit upon the like of him again," said the dealer hurriedly, as he passed me on his other avocations. "Better not lose him, sir; he's well known at Batty's, and they'll have him in the circus again, if they see him. Wish you saw him with his forelegs on a table, ringing the bell for his breakfast."

"I'll take him by the week; though probably a day or two will be all I shall need."

"Four hundred and twelve for Mr. Potts," Dycer screamed out. "Shoes removed and to be ready in the morning."

And so he started on his adventures, this Tartarin of the suburbs. He tells us that his father was a respectable

[3]

apothecary in Saint Mary's Abbey, Dublin, and I expect that Potts was born in that most blameless of Dublin suburbs, Rathmines (where I pen these lines). On the night of his first day's adventure he found himself at dinner with a distinguished company. The subliminal Potts was evoked. He gave a long historical account of his family, mentioning that they came originally from Corsica, and that the name Potts was a corruption of Pozzo, and that they were of the same stock as the celebrated diplomatist Pozzo di Borgo. The unclaimed family estates in the island were of fabulous value, but in asserting his right to them he should have to accept thirteen mortal duels, the arrears of a hundred and one years unscored off. It was in anticipation of these duels that he had taken lessons from Angelo in fencing, which led to the celebrated challenge that the company might have read in *Galignani*, where he offered to meet any swordsman in Europe for ten thousand napoleons, giving choice of the weapon to his adversary. He spoke of a French colonel that he had killed at Sedan, and he incidentally mentioned that he had invented the rifle called after Minié's name. He talked about bear shooting, and mentioned the Emperor of Russia, poor dear Nicholas, and told how they had once exchanged horses, his being more strong-boned and a weight-carrier, whereas the Emperor's was a light Caucasian mare of purest breed, "the dam of that creature you may see below in the stable now." The Emperor had said at parting, "Come and see me one of these days, Potts, and pass a week with me at Constantinople." This was the first intimation he had ever given of his project against Turkey. When Potts told it to the Duke, Wellington made no reply at the time, but he muttered "Strange fellow, Potts—knows everything.". . . But Potts is no Huckleberry Finn, spinning schoolboy falsehoods as he goes along. He is Everyman fighting against fortuitous obscurity. "And if Pitt, why not Potts!" Changing the names, have we not all uttered the same cry? He gets to the Continent and rambles through fiefs that Bismarck and Cavour have not yet made into undistinguishable parts of modern states. He is mistaken for an embassy official, and then for a royal prince travelling incognito. He makes a journey with the strollers, Vaterchen and Catinka, and gets locked up in an Austrian fortress. No, he does not marry little Catinka, the strolling player. We leave him in peace with Kate Herbert or Mary Crofton—one cannot distinguish between these Victorian ladies. But before he left the Continent he saw Catinka again. In her jewelled hand she was holding a piece of sugar to the old circus-horse. She declined to recognise Potts, for she was now the Princess Ernest Maximilian of Württemberg.

After all, perhaps Lever was right in bringing Algernon Sydney to Wales and espousing him to Kate Herbert or Mary Crofton. I can see him in the circus ring, but I can also see him in a seaside place in Victorian times. He lived in a house that had bay windows, and he walked down to the pier with a big telescope under his arm. He would lift it perhaps, and look wistfully after a packet-boat that was crossing to France. Yes, and

A Half-Day's Ride or Estates in Corsica

Mrs. Potts would feel herself getting hot and cold when she remembered the dreadful moment when Algernon Sydney brought the vagabonds, Vaterchen and Catinka, into the drawing-room where she and the ambassador's aunt were having tea.

"A Day's Ride, a Life's Romance" is a history—not, indeed, a skilful history, nor a consistent history, nor an unfailingly successful history—of the pretender that is in all of us. It has a reality, and we remember it when we have forgotten more brilliant, more accomplished, and more profound books. Algernon Sydney Potts was an heroic pretender; he resolutely refused to limit himself to his own bare identity. "Play Macbeth in a paletot," he says, "perform Othello in peg-tops, and see what effect you will produce." He remarks that when a prisoner, sentenced to a long captivity, is no longer addressed by his name, but is simply called 18 or 43, the shock seems to kill the sense of identity, and does much to produce that stolid air of indifference that is characteristic of prison life. In the same way he was affected, he tells us, when he was limited to his Potts nature.

But still another idea can be read into "A Day's Ride," an idea that one could write a novel around or build a play upon: change a factor in your diurnal life and you change your world. In his time there was nothing extraordinary in a young man hiring a mount and going from place to place on horseback. But in Algernon Sydney Potts's case it was a departure; it was non-habitual. The mounting of the horse in Dycer's Yard brought him immediately into a new world—a world that had no relation to the world of respectable apothecaries in Saint Mary's Abbey. He became a candidate for romantic experience as soon as he adopted a non-habitual outlook. The rest of us could change our world if we made as much of an effort—if, say, we go to bed at night and get up in the morning instead of going to bed in the morning and getting up at night; if we would get a Zulu to give us instruction in the throwing of the assagai; or if we rhymesters would take the advice that one Irish bard tendered another—

> Drop the bard and stop the punster,
> Let the quill stay on the goose;
> Take a business trip through Munster,
> Shoot a landlord—be of use!

Myself, I have resolved—well, now and again—to break through my habitual round by going to places that my friends don't take me to and by reading books that nobody wants me to read. I make this resolve in the city that Algernon Sydney Potts started from. Possibly I shall write an account of my discoveries. (As if I don't have to! Here am I imitating Potts, talking as if I expected the public to believe that I own estates in Corsica.) Here is where Dycer's Yard was. *Allons!*

WAXWORKS AND OPERA

Again I am at Madame Tussaud's Exhibition. And it happens again as it happened on former occasions—"We are closing in a quarter of an hour," and saying this the doorman intimates that the establishment includes a cinema in which I can get a more prolonged entertainment. It must be that I have an inner conviction that waxworks belong to the night-life of humanity, and that they cannot work their proper spell if looked at before ten o'clock p.m. Invariably I get to Madame Tussaud's a quarter of an hour before closing time.

I get a ticket from the young lady whose escort is already on hand; I dash madly upstairs to meet an attendant who indicates some noteworthy group that there may be time for me to look at. And then I am immobilized before a group of immobilized beings all bearing illustrious names—a cabinet meeting, or an execution, a gathering of royalties, or a court in which a judge is passing sentence. The attendant has withdrawn, other visitors have departed, and I have the sense of being a solitary witness of the Last Judgment. I hear a whistle blow and a bell ring to warn stragglers that the time is near for them to leave the halls, and I wonder at myself for being so slack as never to give myself the hours in which I could view in

[8]

Waxworks and Opera

its totality an exhibition which is more instructive
than an encyclopedia, more summary than the cate-
chism, more appalling than the crimes in a provincial
newspaper, more curious than a history of the Caesars.
And thinking about the Caesars, I remember that there
was one of them—Domitian, if I remember aright—
who used to banquet his friends in a pitch-black room,
lighted with lamps such as hang in tombs, the service
being rendered by blackened boys who wore demons'
masks. How that Emperor would have gloried in the
Waxworks!

I am seized with a panic, for it becomes likelier and
likelier that I shall leave London without seeing more
than a fractional part of what are the most perfect
Waxworks that have existed in the whole history of
Waxworks. I shall not be able to visit the Chamber of
Horrors. But I make a stand before the very images
of certain famous men and women, having the very
shapes and lengths of their noses, the very size of their
collars, the very shine of their shoes. In the case of a
writer whom the most imperfect-sighted of men could
identify as Rudyard Kipling, I know that the ico-
nographer has counted and rendered the very hairs on
his head no less than the actual index of the glasses
that he wears. Are the names of these wonderful iconographers ever known? If I examined closely the image
of Mr. Hoover or M. Clemenceau should I find a name
where one finds the name of a sculptor in a piece in a
gallery? But I prefer not to find it. I suspect that these
perfect iconographers are the perpetuators of a craft

or mystery that it is well to keep at a distance from. There must be something of the magician in a man who can create a semblance to a particular human being, emphasising with every lifelike detail the rigour of death, the immobility that is the nightmare of all the living. These adepts, whoever they are, are counterfeiters of men; they glory in letting us see how easy it is to remove every ideal gesture and expression from humanity, to withdraw every essence that makes us kindred to what is timeless, to imprison an identity forever in a single circumstance, putting us in three dimensions instead of in the innumerable dimensions that we live, move, and have our being in. But as I reach to these thoughts I notice that one of the homunculi is lifting a warning hand, is opening a mouth. "Time, gentleman, time," he says. He is really a living being, and he is ordering me off the premises. I go.

The Waxworks and the Opera—these are opposites. The Waxworks reflect our morbidity and should have horror for their essential note. And the Opera? I look towards the building in the centre of Paris that has winged and uplifted figures on its roof, with its entrance columns surmounted with eagles, and I see it as a place for magnificent receptions. The Opera reflects our delight in a quickened and graceful social life: it should have gallantry for its essential note. The men in the audience—a number of them—should have decorations and uniforms; the women should be elegant, of course; there should be poets in the audience, but only poets who are famous; they should be courtly, or else have a

hint of desperation about them—they should not be the
kinds of poets who smoke pipes and laugh hoarsely.
Opera is the metropolitan version of the masques that
were produced in courts and castles: it should never be
quite dissociated from royalty and the court. Opera is
Society's night out.

The music, of course, should be good, and so should
the artistry of the performers. But nothing that holds
the mirror up to nature, or purifies through pity or terror, or does any of the things that great art is supposed
to do for us. The piece should be a fairy-tale, but the
sort of fairy-tale that one could tell to an Emperor.
There should be long intervals in which to pay visits to
boxes, to promenade, to look at celebrities, to converse
with brilliant and beautiful friends, to watch people
make dazzling appearances on the great stairway.

And now I am standing within the great entrance
watching the arrival of ladies whose nationality I guess
from their eyes, or their fashion of wearing their wraps
or their jewelry. They are all lovely and elegant this
evening of April. And then I am where statues make
encirclements—busts of singers and composers; they
personify the music that the figures on the roof suggest.
And here are the functionaries who have the appearance
of being high military and civic officials, and others
who wear chains that make them look like the chancellors
of universities. I am made to realize that the prestige
of the Opera is bound up with that of the French state
—the prestige is not to be infringed upon.

I had arranged to meet a friend inside the Opera

House; we had taken adjoining seats. He is at the meeting-place but in a disconsolate state. The Chancellors will not let him go up the grand stairway. My friend is of gypsy stock, and he shows his descent by his apparel—he never has on a collar and tie, and he wears a shirt of heavy red material. But he is a singularly imposing-looking person. Well, in his costume he cannot get admittance. When I hear of the difficulty I order him to don his overcoat and turn up the collar. I do the same myself. Then we present ourselves to the other Chancellors. They are not to be imposed upon. We promise that we will keep to the upper part of the house and not show ourselves in the foyer in the intervals. The promise gains us nothing. My friend they dismiss. Me they treat as a suspiciously bulky-looking person is treated when he tries to pass a customs-barrier. They open my overcoat. My dress just passes. Alone I go up the grand stairway to mingle with the obviously distinguished and presentable people who are on the way to their loges.

The golden horseshoe with its tiers and tiers of people is still; there is not a cough, not a snuffle in that conclave of people. It is a well of stillness after the turmoil of the streets. Naturally I think of Owen Meredith's "Aux Italiens"—a night at the Opera is perfectly expressed in that kind of verse—

> And I turned and looked. She was sitting there
> In a dim box, over the stage ; and dressed
> In that muslin dress with that full soft hair,
> And that jasmine in her breast!

Waxworks and Opera

I was here; and she was there;
  And the glittering horseshoe curved between—
From my bride-betrothed, with her raven hair
  And her sumptuous scornful mien,

To my early love, with her eyes downcast,
  And over her primrose face the shade
(In short from the Future back to the Past),
  There was but a step to be made.

It is all in it—the beauty who "looked like a queen in a
book that night," and who "with the wreath of pearl
in her raven hair" had a "sumptuous scornful mien."
But now the opera is beginning. It is "William Tell"
with my compatriot, John Sullivan, as Arnold. Any
story or any play in which a man bends a bow and
shoots an arrow is a good story or play, as far as I am
concerned: William Tell shooting the apple off his
son's head is a situation to hold any audience; it certainly holds the audience in the Paris Opera House.
Then, for some reason, I am out of the circle before the
rest of the audience. I stand by myself on the grand
stairway. Before me is the most wonderful sight of all
—the Avenue de l'Opéra as I see it through some window, with its hundred thousand lights stretching away,
and around me the great uncrowded structure—the
Opera House whose corridors and colonnades will soon
be filled with Society on its night out.

MISS EUROPE

WOULD that I could write this in French, for then I could begin with an evocative phrase such as I find in an article written by a colleague of mine—"nineteen young visages smiling in the mirror of their destiny." In that style one could write about the election of Miss Europe. But I cannot be evocative: I can only be historical. . . . Nineteen middle-aged jurymen. . . .

To be absolutely historical, only eighteen jurymen, for one of the jury was a lady. Nineteen of a jury, one for every nation that sent a candidate for election, met in the salle of *Le Journal* office. We had a conference. It was as solemn as a cabinet meeting. How should the young ladies who were to present themselves be garbed? That was the first question to be decided. Bathing-dresses were suggested. But that suggestion was immediately rejected by the president of the jury, a celebrated painter. Bathing-dresses were disfiguring; the candidates would have to be judged as *femmes nues* or *femmes sociales*—there was nothing between. *Femmes nues*, pronounced the president. (He was a man who looked like an English prime-minister of the eighteen-nineties—like Lord Salisbury). But, said the editor in charge of the competition, young ladies of good society do not show themselves undressed. The president looked as if he had heard this before, but did not quite understand the scruple. It would be judgment based on incomplete evidence. However . . . *femmes sociales* if we would have it so. The young ladies, then, were to appear dressed as in drawing-rooms. But their legs would have to be shown at some stage of the proceedings.

So we took our seats at the green-covered tables, an international jury of nineteen. It was made up of painters and sculptors. I, so that I might have some association with the visible arts, was put down as *critique d'art*. Seen from our stalls in the *salle du Journal*, how remote was the unpleasantness that was rife in Europe some years ago. France and Germany, Italy and Austria, Bulgaria and Roumania, Greece and Turkey, and the countries that had other names then, and the countries that were only war-fronts, had declared solemnly that they would never, never speak to each other again, and here they were, all ready to be enchanted with a beauty brought from some former enemy land! Another point: this jury whose range was from the Bosphorus to the North Sea, these young ladies who were from so many lands, had all a European manner, a European idiom. It was not merely that their communication in French was natural and easy; it was that they all seemed to have a like background. There were two exceptions—Miss Angleterre and Miss Irlande: they were more remote from the European style than were Miss Bulgarie and Miss Turquie: they were both provincials.

Beside this was to be set the non-appearance of national types. We were startled when Miss Espagne presented herself: here was race; what we had been looking at before was the common denominator of Caucasianism. Then Miss Grèce showed race, Miss Hollande, and Miss Irlande. As for the rest, they might just as easily have come out of Denmark as out of France, out of Poland as out of Roumania, out of Germany as out of Czechoslovakia, out of Belgium as out of Italy. Leaving out one candidate, the good looks of those presenting themselves could be equalled by the pick of an American finishing school.

Here were eighteen decidedly pretty girls. But I had seen just as many of the same degree of prettiness at commencement exercises at more than one school in the United States. That unmarked variety of type could be found, too, in an American school. With the exception of the four distinctive types, I had seen all of them in some American school.

The candidates entered one by one, in the alphabetical order of their countries. Allemagne was first. She was the German girl of to-day while Autriche was the German girl of yesterday—the one, boyish, short-haired, blue-eyed, with dimples which she readily displayed, and the other with the clear forehead behind which, one guessed, she lived a good deal—blonde, intelligent, and reserved. Bulgarie and Turquie had the honest charm, the sweet and winning look of girls who come out of worthy households—nothing specious and nothing exotic about them. Russie, Roumanie, Belgique, Yougoslavie, Pologne, were society girls such as one sees at the opera. Danemark was heroic and well-featured; France, who was nearly as tall and as blonde as Danemark, had no particular charm. Hongrie had not the vividness of the Hungarian type; Angleterre and Irlande had poor sense of the situation; Italie looked as if she had on the silver wig that the loverless girl in the Venusberg wore when "Tannhäuser" was on at the Opera; she and Tchécoslovaquie had cinema faces and moved as if they were mannequins. Hollande had something spontaneous and spring-like about her, yet one could know her for a Dutch maiden—she was the most girlish of the beauties. Espagne had much too much sense of the situation: she displayed her ear-rings and the flower on her shoulder, and she almost made us see a fan in her hand; no national costumes were worn, but Espagne gave us the impression that she had one on. All the candidates had the right manner—a mixture of self-possession and modesty, of friendliness and reserve. How apt socially girls are in comparison with young men!

The jury marked on three points giving a maximum of three for each point—head, body, general vivaciousness. As she entered, the candidate went up to each of the jury, smiled, said a word, received a compliment. Then she went on a platform. She turned her head, raised her arms as directed. Then she exhibited her legs to the knees. What might be termed the village-beauty group were embarrassed at this stage: Madame, the wife of the editor who had arranged the competition, tucked up their skirts for them. The girls who belonged to high society, or who had connections with the theatre or the studio, showed no embarrassment. Miss Hollande laughed delightfully as if she were up to some prank. Miss Espagne seemed to say, "Here are my legs; there's nothing wrong with them." Miss France showed her garters as well as her knees.

The intelligent reader will have noticed that I have barely spoken of Miss Grèce. Her photograph, as were the photographs of the others, was on the sheet before us, and we knew that her head had the classic line. She entered, and we saw that with the beauty we expected she had something else. There was something thorough-bred about her, like a small Arab horse. She had racial distinctiveness. She had elegance. She was dressed to perfection. She flirted with us. But, unlike Miss Es-pagne's, hers was no cabaret flirtation. Asphodels blos-somed round us.

Imagine a dark-skinned and very slender girl sheathed in silver: the features were like those on a medallion, her hair in a knot on her neck. When I say "dark-skinned" I am, perhaps, too emphatic: I suppose her skin was really olive. When she stood upon the platform and raised her arms, or held back her head, or turned a hand, she took, naturally and simply, the lines of a tanagra or painting on a vase. Dividing her long silver skirt she showed her legs to the knees. She did this so charmingly that I, for one, felt like applauding as one applauds when one sees a surprisingly graceful gesture in the ballet. She seemed to say to us "In the Peloponnesus there is still a remnant of the Hellenic race. I happen to be that survival. I am sure, messieurs, you are delighted to come so close to the most aristocratic type that Europe has produced. And I can respond— I am responding to you." She thanked us and left the jury-room.

I looked down the line and knew that the verdict would go to this representative of the classic type. I repeated to myself a sentence from one of the Kai Lung books: "The most celebrated painters of the province, having observed the unstudied grace of her move-ments, threw away the implements of their craft and became trainers of performing elephants." We marked our papers. The six who had received the highest num-ber of votes came in together and stood upon the plat-form—they made a charming group as they talked to each other and arranged one another's dresses and hair. At a word from the President they withdrew. We wrote a single name on our paper and handed it in. I am not sure that the election of Miss Grèce was unanimous. But if votes went to any of her rivals they were no more than three or four. She was recalled; the jury stood up to receive her. I did not repent of my vote; she was beautiful, whereas the others, at their best, were only pretty. But she had flaws. Her mouth was too firm, and those dark eyes of hers were neither deep nor lu-minous; they were shallow, smouldering eyes. Also, this young lady was much too much at home in the world. She went to the President and made a graceful speech of thanks. Going to each of the jury, she per-mitted her hand to be kissed. *"Merci bien, monsieur, merci bien.*" Then this silver-clad, slender, classic beauty left us. Miss Grèce was Miss Europe; Europe had gone back to the classical.

> On desperate seas long wont to roam,
>   Thy hyacinth hair, thy classic face,
> Thy Naiad airs have brought me home
>   To the glory that was Greece . . .

But when I repeated the verse, I knew I was wrong. This was no Nausicaa, no young Helen, no young Clytemnestra. Neither Attica nor Sparta was her land. When the Emperors born in the purple would take a bride, they sent their emissaries through the Byzantine dominions to find the loveliest that the city or the village, the hut or the palace could show, and had the diadem placed upon her head, making her co-ruler of the Imperial world. Her mothers had lived in expectation of the call that would raise them beside the Autocrator. That was the reason she had looked upon us as if we were monks and emperors. She was not Hellenic but Byzantine; not Nausicaa nor Helen, but Theodora or Theophano. Europe had gone back to Byzance.

MY FRIENDS THE MIDGETS

WILL you or nill you, when you go third-class you are member of a community. Travel first or second and you don't have to push along corridors or crowd in and out of dining-rooms. But for us who are neither first- nor second-class, the liner is a promenade, a camp and a compound all strung together. This evening, at set of sun, a flock of us coming from feeding spread over the lower deck, settled down on hatchments, hopped up on chairs and boxes, and fluttered up ladders to a higher deck: then one felt like a rook in a most populous rookery.

But who would stay with the first- or second-class passengers when the third-class decks show such varied life? Here are negroes throwing dice: forgetful of their Aryan accomplishment they moan the syllables of the forest—"Ah, ah, ah," as they follow the throw. A turbaned East Indian, undistracted, reads a Persian book. An Armenian speaks of prices in Damascus. A bald-headed mulatto postures for a spectacular boxing-match. A tall Scandinavian watches the sea with the eyes of a Viking. Forward there is another third-class deck: compared with the quarters we frequent there is something unsocial in its bare boards crossed with iron pieces. Men stand solitary there like captives or hostages beside iron pillars, or they move about as in a wide cage. I am not surprised to hear the barking of animals in this hardly inhabited hemisphere. A pack of poodles are being fed oranges on the bare deck.

But it was on this deck that I became friendly with Karl and Franz. Where had they come from? "The Harz Mountains," one said, and the other added, "where the canaries come from." I allowed my fancy to play with the idea that the Harz Mountain habitants were all midget-sized and were all occupied with the raising of canaries. But that was too good to be true. There was a difference of four years between Franz and Karl and in the interval was born that tall brother of theirs, Wilhelm, who, bursting out of the suit he has on, still seems to be growing. Wilhelm, half policeman, half showman, must be as typical of the Harz Mountaineers as Franz or Karl.

Fantastic as the beasts on a clipped hedge the poodles eat and roll their oranges. The lady of the poodles has Franz and Karl on a bench beside her. With her benevolent intent she looks like Swift's one sympathetic character, and I might be seeing in life an illustration for "Gulliver's Travels" were it not for the fact that there are two Gullivers beside this Brobdingnagian. Karl wears glasses; he has a serious, not to say troubled countenance, and the hair is smooth on the flat top of his head. Both wear a little ring on a finger. Karl's is amethyst, and this in conjunction with his serious expression gives him an episcopal look. Franz's face is free of solemnity, but it is a little peaked; his hair goes

My Friends the Midgets

up in a plume. Both laugh easily, but while Karl's is in cackles Franz's laugh goes in chimes.

What ages are they? Speaking to myself and the lady of the poodles and the two nuns who are seated at the back and who are enormously interested and entertained, Wilhelm states that their actual ages are forty-four and forty-eight, their professional ages are twenty and twenty-four, and their train ages are eight and twelve. Karl and Franz nod smilingly at this statement of chronology. A train-conductor looking at them in a berth and being informed by Wilhelm that they had under-age tickets remarked, "They may be eight and twelve, but I've been seeing these boys for the past twenty years." Karl cackled and Franz's laugh went in chimes, Madame smiled sympathetically, and the nuns swayed with silent laughter. The "boys" do vaudeville turns on the Continent and in England and America.

They have nothing either shrinking or assertive about them; they are urbane; they are even men of the world. They have not, I judge, any consciousness of isolation from normal-sized humanity. Probably this is because they have always had a family life: they are two together and they have always had big Wilhelm whose interest is their interest and who can jolly them along. Wilhelm is their entrepreneur. "It's extraordinary the questions people will ask about the 'boys,'" Wilhelm says. "Women especially. Even well-educated women will ask the queerest questions." But there was nothing abnormal about their mother and father. There were children who grew to normal size. Then there was Karl

who ceased to grow when he was three. Then there were
other normal-sized children. Then there was Franz.
After some other children of normal growth there was
a girl who remained midget-sized. She is still living in
the Harz Mountains: she does not go round with the
"boys." "It's not good for a woman to be in this business of ours," Karl remarks sententiously.

When in Franz's case cessation in growth was noticed he was taken to an institution in some near-by
city. There a great specialist observed him. But one day
Franz got hold of a big bottle of Rhine wine and drank
all of it. He fell down unconscious, and a message was
sent home that he was dead. His father went to take
the body home, bringing a little coffin on his cart. When
he arrived Franz was frisking about. Then Franz rode
home. I could see that progress with Franz seated on the
top of the coffin and his hair rising in a plume. The
story draws sympathetic exclamations from the nuns
and an indulgent look from the lady of the poodles.

Wilhelm, having got into the vein, tells us more
about Franz and Karl. They do a prize-fighting act in
their vaudeville: there is a furious contest, refereed by
Wilhelm, in which Karl gets a knock-out. Their pub-
licity-man had the fight prohibited; the governor of the
state was induced to attend, and after watching the
first round, to forbid the brutal spectacle. When the
fight was announced as being on again Franz was ar-
rested and landed in a cell. As soon as the turnkey's
back was turned he slipped out between the bars; the
news of his escape was broadcast. As the story ended

we heard Karl's cackling and Franz's chimes, the nuns swayed themselves delightedly and Madame softly laughed.

Then there was the story of Karl and the elephant. Wilhelm, as he brought the "boys" on to the platform, used to give a piece of cake to an elephant that was somewhere by. He gave up handing out cake, and, as he passed he would wave the waiting elephant away. The elephant decided to get at Wilhelm through one of his charges, and when Karl was hurrying to join the the pair who had gone before, the elephant levelled at him a trunk filled with water and sawdust and covered him over with the stuff. As it was told, the grave Karl enacted the incident—the shock, his prostration, his scrambling up to get on with the show, and his defiance of the resentful elephant.

He stands while Franz helps Madame to intern her poodles and Wilhelm attends the nuns on their way back to the other deck. He is solemn as he looks out on the sea. To him, too, life must be a dilemma, and probably he is not always able to turn on the resentful elephants with the defiance he has exhibited for us.

Here, away from the promenade, the camp, and the compound, it is good to watch the night come down. The figures moving on the bare deck become like shadows: then, feeling the loneliness of their quarter, they leave the deck and pass through the depths of the ship to its more inhabited parts. There they find movement and conversation, music and drinks. Now the liner seems like some unexplained structure in a scientific romance: she moves as a ship, but what we have been taught to look for on a ship—a captain and sailors— are nowhere present. There are masses of iron on the deck, but we feel that these are survivals merely, like the arms of a whale, things that have ceased to be organic. Ceaselessly, imperturbably, the vessel holds a course over the dark ocean. And that expanse of water furrowed by the flowing river that follows the ship restores to us the planetary sense: we are climbing across a planet with a moon for an index of a wider expanse. On a high mast, far up, a little lamp hangs. One cannot believe that this light has any utility—it is probably like the wonderfully coloured jars in the pharmacist's window, or like the lamp in a cathedral—a symbolic light.

The poodles being kennelled, Franz and Madame seat themselves side by side. The broad face bends down on the peaked little face with a deal of tenderness. Madame is Flemish; she has only the symbols of giantism—a white rose, extravagant in the size of its petals, on the shoulder of her red dress, ear-rings that are like miniature towers of gold, and a necklace that seems inordinately wide because it is of coral alternating with bands of metal. She smiles as she listens to Franz's flow of talk.

But on the third-class decks we have a propriety-remembrancer (he is the interpreter, a Frenchman), and at ten o'clock he comes with his appeal, "Now, bonny lassies." This is to segregate the young women, and induce them to leave these open, darkening spaces, and go

My Friends the Midgets

below. Madame heeds the proprieties; she takes leave of Franz.

Later I come upon my friends in another part of the ship. They are at a table with seidels of beer before them and cigars in their mouths. The cigar that each has is the length of his arm from fingers to elbow. But they take no more time than anybody else in consuming them. I hear Karl call for a cannibal sandwich.

A piece of machinery that we thought was inorganic begins to function, winding a massive cable out of the depths of the ship. Our port is near. We are left to watch the lights on the ship and the lights on the shore. The pilot is coming on board! An oil-lamp is lowered, and, amid some eager applause, the pilot with his handbag comes up on our liner. In the lowering of the obsolete lamp, in the eager welcome to the pilot, there is something of ancient ceremony.

And when it is light again the ship moves along the docks, past high stages filled with watchers. Man after man, woman after woman, picks out a friend on the ship and makes a sign of welcome. One man stands rigid and intent, searching every yard of the nearing ship. No movement around can make him change his position. Intent, leaning forward with gaunt face, he searches, searches for somebody of whom he despairs. The ship comes nearer and goes past him, and no sign of recognition has moved his clenched hands and bloodless face. The gangway is pushed across. Karl and Franz, led by Wilhelm, go before me. They waddle; the legs of these little men are not for marching.

A MARRIAGE IN MANHATTAN

Twenty couples with their coadjutors waited for an alderman who would perform the marriage ceremony, and gaiety lived through their tedium. The scene suggested an O. Henry story; however, I could not think of what opening it should have. I turned to the bridegroom whose witness I was and mentioned this difficulty. He looked at the waiting couples seated on chairs and benches, examined the notices, one of which said, "Marriages absolutely free," and the other, "Do not spit," and presented me with this opening, "The place lacked a bar and a free lunch counter."

Gaiety survived our tedium, but we began to look for distractions. There was a narrow window between the solid pillars of the Manhattan City Hall; we could see the snow falling like white dust, and a brawny team striving with a wagon. The bridegroom who sat with the dignified negro lady began to make motions with his hands as if to rattle and cast dice. The Syrian whispered to his witnesses that they might begin to tell stories. But a young woman had opened her bag and was showing scraps of patterns to her friends. Suddenly a pair of silk stockings that matched her wedding dress unrolled. We all forgot the particular distraction we were bent on, so entertained were we by this episode.

And now a basilisk-eyed young man stood at the door

of the anteroom and surveyed us. Was he the alderman's orderly? If so, we would not be disappointed in our hopes of marrying and giving in marriage that day. But the basilisk-eyed young man was not the orderly. "He's a reporter, come to get a human-interest story," said a bridegroom who knew the journals. He got nothing out of us. His mind was already made up that the human interest amongst us was negligible. He failed even to notice "The Kid."

We knew her as "The Kid" before we knew her as "Number 27." "Which of them is 'The Kid' going to marry?" some curious person had said in the office below where you pay a dollar for your license to marry—the office that is opposite the coroner's room. Then she was one in a conference on a document that is entitled "State of New York Affidavit for License to Marry." She chewed gum and swung her legs while her head was on the shoulder of one young man and her arm round the neck of another. "Kid" was a good name for this young Manhattanese: she had the sprightliness and unexpectedness of the goat young; she had the fair hair and the blue eyes of the human young. "The alderman isn't paid for marrying you—he does it at his own convenience," the official said to the two young men when they went to his bureau. "He may come in at half-past three, and he mayn't come here at all. But if you want to wait go upstairs to room so and so." The young men told her this, and she bobbed out of the room with them; I thought that by this time she was on some other slope of Manhattan.

A Half-Day's Ride or Estates in Corsica

But here she was in the anteroom to the alderman's office. She provided for the rest of us an entertainment that was partly light character comedy and partly a moving-picture show. She chewed gum with zest and swung her legs as if she were on a trapeze in mid-air. She made wide eyes at what one youth said and covered her face with her hands at what another told her. Her collar was hitched up, and it was plain that she had learnt the trick of carrying her coat from "one of the boys." Blue was the color she displayed. The dress under the fawn-colored coat was blue, and the big blue bow at the back of her hat matched the colour of her eyes. "The Kid" was sixteen. The women thought that the hair above the blue eyes was dyed to that fairness.

We decided that the young man who was rather thoughtful and withdrawn was the one whom "The Kid" was going to marry. He looked a steady youth who might become a good provider. But he should have been goat-footed and have had pointed ears. He should have been ready to leap and gambol with her up a mountain-side, and, we, too, should have been more excited about "The Kid." She brought something that was hymeneal into the solid-built City Hall of Manhattan. Even at the threshold of the alderman's office she recalled the dance and the mountain-side. Her skip and her swagger had some memory of the Maenads. Even her yawn was frolicsome.

At last the tipstaff came and gathered us together. He formed us in a queue outside the door of the alderman's office. Then he spoke severely to a negro girl

[30]

A Marriage in Manhattan

who threw herself at the end of the line. "What," said he, "do you want to get married, too?" "Mebbe," she bubbled, impressing a startled-looking colored man to her side. The tipstaff went along the line of grooms and brides and witnesses. He was hollow-eyed and dis-illusioned-looking. "And are you number 27?" said he to "The Kid." She made her blue eyes wide while she chewed her gum and nodded. "Gosh, I wish I was getting you, Number 27," said the tipstaff. Then, with a renunciatory look he went down the line, and opened the door of the alderman's office to the first couple.

Afterwards I saw the blue of her hat as Number 27 skipped down the steps going underground. Number 27! There is little in a name, after all, when a number can remain so evocative.

TRAVEL FILM

In Chicago the elevated railway trains and the surface cars had ceased running; there was a "tie-up." The people waiting in the open spaces of the city looked like crowds watching the course of some disastrous comet. Across bridge beyond bridge crowds marched, and in their full and unvarying lines they suggested the terrifying pictures of the Day of Judgment. Men and women were piled upon big motor trucks, packed into furniture vans, strung along wagons. Policemen on horseback, with stirrups leather-fronted, Mexican or Western fashion, paraded along the lines of the crowd. The great stores were transporting their girl-workers: behind the crates or the steel nets of the motor wagons these young women looked like the spoil of some barbarian conqueror. But Chicagoans, their papers boasted, were taking the "tie-up" in the spirit of the Mardi Gras Carnival in New Orleans. Certainly some of the vehicles that I saw in use looked like fragments of a circus procession.

We make a careful journey to our railway station on a little mule cart that has some chairs placed in it. Just beyond the barrier our train waits. It shows a red disk with white letters upon it—"Overland Limited." Two or three people are in this car or coach, lounging as they would in a waiting-room. A night's journey. Then comes the prairie land. The houses on that flat surface are like pigeon-boxes that someone has left down on the ground. The breaks in the flatness are belts of trees or tangles of shrub on which crows are resting. This is Iowa. Then comes Nebraska. Out of the black earth rise canes that were stalks of maize; they glimmer in the sunlight, canes stuck in the black earth, distances and distances of them. Black and red cattle stand in the fields; brown-red hogs rove about; there are high white towers that are grain-elevators. This is the granary of America; for half a day we hurtle through it without striking a town.

And now no patches with stalks of corn. There are wide, hay-coloured fields with hay-coloured mounds upon them. Sometimes the face of a mound is down and then one sees vivid green within. These are silage heaps. Corn cut in the autumn has been kept green in them; cattle stand around eating into green plenty that has been reserved for them.

A brown table-featured land; colourless trees stand around houses that have yards full of cattle, all motionless and all of the same colour. It is still Nebraska, still an almost unpeopled land. But we are rising and rising. To-night we shall be in the passes of the Rocky Mountains. Meanwhile it is a land that the Cherksas, or whatever name the tribes of the steppes have, might roam across. Night comes down, making the cornstalks in the black earth seem tattered and spectral. The earth is black like the black smoke that goes up from our engine.

The Great Divide! The backbone of America, that which divides the continent! But we crossed it in the night; we are in the foot-hills of the Rockies, and the train is sliding—literally sliding—down into Wyoming and Utah. Down we go, using power only to keep the brakes working. Snow, and out of the hillocks, shrubs with snow on their branches. The details remind one of a Japanese picture, but the landscape is wide, immense. Still, we have crossed the Great Divide, and the Orient begins to touch upon us. The gangs of men that we see along the permanent way are Japanese, and there are many Japanese farmers and farm-labourers about this part of Wyoming.

M— called me to look at something she had discovered. Chinese babies, no less. They are in a bunk, watched over by their young mother—babies of old ivory, with round, chubby wrists and jewel-like eyes. They are quiet, wonderfully quiet, and the Chinese mother tells us that they are a boy and a girl, one a few months and the other over a year old. When we pass again the mother is laughing and cooing over them. Does anything more than a metaphysical smile ever come to the lips of a Chinese baby, I wonder. When we see them again, an ancient Chinaman with American clothes on him, and a million wrinkles on his face, is tending the babies. Very patient he is with them. We ask what the baby's name is. "George," he tells us. And the girl-baby's? "Rose."

Travel Film

"Utah welcomes you," a station-sign takes on itself to say. So we are out of Wyoming and in a country that at least has a story—the heroic and crazy story of Brigham Young and the Mormon beginnings. I liked Utah for that first glimpse of it—a swift river running through snow, and mountain-peaks around. And then a great lake, a whole sea, with cloud-white peaks and rugged iron-looking ramparts bounding it. Over a bridge that crossed the lake our train ran—for over thirty minutes it kept straight across. And then we were in the strangest land I had ever looked on.

Empty it was as our thought of Siberia. Flat it was, like a lake's surface covered with snow. But up through the snow, sage bushes and patches of sage bushes stuck. Cold jade was the sky; a gleam of green was cast upon the white mountain-peak. Immense was that flat, tufted, waterless land, with black lines that were our iron tracks going through it. A one-dimensional scene— flatness and lines. The smoke from our train extended in a single line behind, a line lengthening, never breaking, the plume of a monstrous bird. Buttresses and barriers of mountains, and everything else flat. A land for a myth. But what myth might be actionless enough for this empty land with the jade-cold sky above it?

California! Instead of the level of Utah with its strange buttresses, we have clumps of trees here— clumps of trees in a green country. Greener and greener the land grows, and more and more moist. And with its trees that are like arbutuses and with its clouded skies, this part of California looks like Ireland. Along the railway-track are little fires. Tramps stand by them. This railway is the tramp's—or rather, the hobo's—highway. One of them stands to watch the train. He is a Mexican; his upper lip has been eaten away; he has a top-boot on one foot and an ordinary shoe on the other. A pack is on his back. He stands there, gross and glum. He might be a statue put up to express all the bitterness and defeat of the pioneer.

I do not like the part of California that I sojourn in —the southern part. Here the people and the landscape are in open disharmony—the landscape says one thing, the people and the buildings they put up say something quite different. I have an apprehension that there is nothing integral here. In Los Angeles (did ever a city have a name so foreign to it?) I see health and well-being. But I think I should have to go a long way through its streets to encounter a human being who could understand the desperate virtues of Faith, Hope and Charity. And yet I saw people pray very earnestly in this City of the Angels. But it was in a little Mexican chapel. Hollywood, I suppose, has done much to sap whatever was spiritually or morally strenuous in this place. The girls who have made themselves over to look like movie-actresses—and all shop-girls, stenographers, and telephone-operators have done this—add to the effect of unreality, of something unmoored in the lives of the inhabitants of this bright city. Most of these girls have come this far to try to get into the studios: they have had to take ordinary jobs in the city, but they look, dress, think, and behave as if they thought

themselves understudies for the queens of the cinema.
Then there are the girls who can sit for hours and hours
and hours in the lobbies of the hotels: statuary in mu-
seums is not more inanimate than they can be——their
only motion is when they make use of a lip-stick. For
what do they wait? For the chance of meeting some
man who will ask them to lunch or take them for a
motor-ride.

But I should not imply that I found no high serious-
ness in Los Angeles. There was that Indian whom I saw
showing riding-feats; a very old Indian he was, but he
did what he offered to do as if his whole life depended
upon his doing it with thoroughness and finish; I like
seeing a man doing difficult things in such a way. I
wrote some verses about him which I will set down
here——

> The swiftness that you won in the death-chase,
> Out on the plains, five hundred moons ago,
> The hardness wrought of hungers, and the skill
> That notched that hardness, arrow to that bow;
>
> You show us these, while these depart from you
> Like warriors softly shod, with bodies bent,
> Passing a mesa-bluff around which howl
> Coyotes, the beasts of discontent.

There was also the man who had the tattooing establishment and who talked to me passionately and in-
structively about his mystery. He would have im-
printed some of his fine designs on me: he had ones ap-

propriate for my wrists and my arms, my back and my chest. But his offerings were not, as the American editors say, available: I should have had to remain some time in Los Angeles to have myself tattooed with any richness of design. This tattooer had a little workshop on the outskirts of the city; upon the walls, outside and inside, were hung the cartoons which his needle would work out on men's flesh: they had the stiffness of elaboration, the elemental grotesqueness of ancient Mexican pictures. (I am sure that all who have studied both tattooing and Aztec art have noted that when the first is pictorial it has affinities with the second.) I admired all his designs; they had not only significant form but significant colour; particularly I admired a blue spouting whale which could have gone very nicely between my shoulders or on my chest. But above all, I admired his interest in and his devotion to the ancient and lasting art, which has not been feminized and which is patronized only by the most masculine of he-men.

I went to Hollywood. I went into a studio as big as the concourse of the Grand Central Terminal. A castle was in one corner, a Tibetan settlement was in another, a Western cowboy drama was being enacted in the middle. The director to whom I had been presented was registering a dinner-table scene in another nook. The guests were at table, all looking so much like poor relations that my sympathy for them was heartfelt. Their drill went on for hours and hours. However, the studio had its entertainer. He was a troubadour who went from castle to ranch, from village to dining-room: he sang and he played a guitar, and I was very much interested to find a recrudescence of minstrelsy in these ultramodern surroundings. And then I was presented to the doll-like little lady for whom, as somebody thought, I could write something. She was nice to me, but her mind was engaged on other matters. I told her I would make a trip to the atolls of the South Seas and then come back and give myself the pleasure and profit of attending on her. I think she thought that this was quite an ordinary thing to do. So I left Hollywood. The fragrance of the orange flowers was on the ways to the studio when I came back; the humming-birds had crossed the Gulf and were vibrant before the flowers. I saw the doll-like little lady. She told me the story I was to write for her. It was quite a good story. Only if I were to write it I should be liable for prosecution for plagiarism by a writer whose book had sold in millions of copies.

A VISIT TO MADAME PELE

W E WASHED the dishes after our picnic supper; we locked the door of the cottage that had been loaned to us, and then—our casualness seems incredible to me now—we went off to visit Madame Pele.

But you do not know who Madame Pele is. She is a goddess, and the most manifest of goddesses. Said an old Hawaiian lady whom we saw on another island, "That was when we worshipped stones and Madame Pele," and her tone implied that she had a certain worshipful feeling for her still. Pele was the fire-goddess of these volcanic islands: she was thought of as living in the crater of the volcano Ki-lau-ea. But the distinction between the goddess and the place she lived in has been lost: Pele now is Ki-lau-ea. And when an Hawaiian speaks of Madame Pele, he means, or she means, the active volcano.

Ours was a very great privilege, for we were going to see Madame Pele at her grandest. We had been given a homesteader's place that was in the actual neighbourhood of the goddess. We had supper there; we washed the dishes and we closed the door, and we went off to make our visit.

Pele's story is the epic of Hawaii. Once, while in her spirit-form, she saw and she loved the handsome prince

A Visit to Madame Pele

Lo-hi-au. She sent her youngest sister Hi-i-aka to fetch the bridegroom to her. And while her sister was still upon her errand Pele broke faith with her. She destroyed the lehua groves that were sacred to Hi-i-aka, and she changed Ho-po-e, Hi-i-aka's friend, into a lehua tree. Hi-i-aka brought Lo-hi-au to her sister's court. But then, seated with him on the ferny brink of the volcano, in revenge for what her sister had done to her, she invited and received the bridegroom's kisses. Then the rage of Pele burst forth. She overwhelmed Lo-hi-au and turned his body into a pillar of rock. She convulsed, land and sea. Indeed, she would have brought the whole world to ruin if it had not been for the intervention of Kane, the Earth-shaper. That was the sort of goddess that Pele was.

Well, on the night of April third, we made our call upon her. And the approach to her court was unforgettable. The double lights of the car showed the giant ferns that bordered the way—ferns fathom high and fathom broad. And then we came out on a level expanse—black and level, a silent sea of lava made up of various flows. Long before that we had seen the red haze that was in the sky above the crater.

Everything in Hawaii has an element of the dramatic. But the sight of Ki-lau-ea in near-eruption is surpassingly dramatic. The molten lava was within three hundred and fifty feet of the top. And what a setting is there for a volcano's activity!

The crater is an open bowl, roughly—not very roughly—circular. The inner court of the Pennsylvania

A Half-Day's Ride or Estates in Corsica

Railway Station in New York would fit within it. And it is open, mind you; one has to climb no peaks and go down through no funnels to it. Around the volcano's fire is a perfect amphitheatre.

And it was this that impressed me most about Kilau-ea—this amphitheatre that one is aware of as one comes up to the volcano—an amphitheatre that is lighted up by a strange theatrical lighting. This lighting would be the triumph of a theatre: it makes the markings within the great bowl appear like seats for a vast and solemn audience—an audience that must remain silent through the mere effect of the lighting—a hushed audience in a great amphitheatre.

Then you look below. There is a surging as of a sea. It is the rising and falling of the fire-fountains, the flowing of the fire-rivers—a sound of continuous surge. There is black and there is molten gold. A great fiery-golden river, with floes of black upon it, goes through the molten black. The floes break and melt away. A fiery mountain rises and falls. Tracks of fiery red go through the blackness. Black and red, red and black are the colours shown below.

The black, as it is lighted up by the fountains that rise out of it and the rivers that flow across it, is as impressive as the fieriness. Dragons of molten gold crawl across it, dragons and serpents. No wonder one thinks of silent spectators in the amphitheatre. For what they are there to look upon is the beginning of creation—the great Fire Play. Look through a telescope at the rivers and fountains, the tracks and the flashes of fire, and you

A Visit to Madame Pele

will believe that you are viewing astronomical phenomena—fires radiating and darting from a planet in the making.

Solemn the amphitheatre seems; it is lighted from below. The red-golden fire rises and falls in fountains upon the floor of blackness; rivers of fire flow, or, like dragons, crawl across it—the floor of molten lava that cracks, melts, and falls away like cakes of ice in a thawing stream.

The night is the proper time to look on all this. But daylight is a time to look again. Before one comes to the crater one sees a great expanse—it looks as if a clearing had been made by giants for the making of a giant's garden. Miles and miles have been levelled; rough clay and earth have been left in mounds upon the clearing, and plants and ferns are carelessly coming up. A terrific clearing! And then one comes upon the lava—a great hard sea of blackness with steam mounting through interstices in it. We go to the pit and look down. The fire is not golden now; it is red—Mephistophelian red, and I realise how sinister fires can look. The fires here are indeed the fires of Mephistopheles—the fires of the Earth Spirit. This is Ka Piko o ka Honua, the navel of the earth. And because it is the navel of the earth Pele chose it for her dwelling-place.

ISLAND DAYS

The Valley Dweller

A MAN is on the road that will bring him by zigzag ways down into a valley. He wears a yellow oilskin and the foot that protrudes out of his wooden stirrup is bare. It rains and he has on a hat of *lau-hala* fibre. We converse in a mixture of English and Hawaiian, the Hawaiian contributed by me being mainly the affirmative and the negative—*pololei* and *aole*. He is a Kanaka pure, he tells me, father Kanaka, mother Kanaka; a Kanaka of the valleys he is. Below are Waipaio's thirteen valleys, all opening on the ocean, and I can see the Pacific making a great frill of lace on the black lava shingles; the hills bear down in gulches furrowed by narrow streams. As we talk, men on horseback come up out of the valley and go down into it; they lead horses carrying high packs; they are bringing down stores or bringing up produce. Below us is a flat marked into different squares by rice and taro patches.

What mixture, I ask myself, is in the Hawaiian blood of the man who speaks to me? A pure Hawaiian would be genial if he spoke in this offhand way; he would laugh with me. But this man smiles only, and as he smiles he looks into my face in a childlike and pathetic way. He talks lengthily, holding his roan horse and with his bare foot through the wooden stirrup. Hawaiians are dramatic, but they are never actors; this man sees himself and is acting a part—he is a play-boy. But the pathos in his eyes and the sense of loneliness that is about him make him no genial play-boy. And he has such an odd personal distinction. Hawaiians have distinction, but it is race distinction, never personal distinction. This man has queer personal distinction—he reminds me of a Spaniard or of a West of Ireland man.

I ask him what people live in the valley. Hawaiian and Chinese, he tells me—thirty Kanaka families, thirty Pake. What do they live on down there? On what they grow—taro, rice. Do the Kanaka grow rice? No, Pake grow rice. They all have fish. And then he speaks of the splendid Hawaiian mullet. The Kanaka have *poi* and fish, nothing else—no tea, no coffee, and now no pig.

He went on to apologise for his inexpressiveness in English. He had been three months at school, and then —*pau*—no more. He tapped his head—not good. On account of his poor brain, he suggested, he had remained poor. "Man no shoe, horse no shoe," he said. He protruded his bare foot and gazed at it pathetically. "Man bare, horse bare," he said.

Then he brightened up. "If you come down," he said, "we give you *poi*, potatoes, fish." As a further inducement, he said *oklehou*—the word is the Hawaiian version of our "alcohol," and signifies a spirit distilled from the *ti*-plant. He added something more. "If you come *wahine hula*"—his wife would show me a *hula*.

A Half-Day's Ride or Estates in Corsica

I thought of a middle-aged Hawaiian woman dancing and I was not fired at the thought. And then I asked him how long he had been married.

"Three months and two days," he said. I asked him what age he was. "Forty-three," he said, and he took off his hat and invited me to regard his grey hairs. There was a sprinkling of them. He looked at me with a wistful, winning, and pathetic smile.

I asked him if he had not been married before.

"Three *wahine* before—four *wahine* altogether," he told me.

Four wives! I expressed astonishment. Perhaps he was dignifying casual connections by suggesting four entrances into matrimony. But he held up his hand solemnly. "I promise. I Christian."

"What kind of Christian?" I ask.

"Christian, Hawaiian style," he says. He meant Mormon, I knew. The Mormons are creating something like a national church for the Polynesians. But the Mormon missionaries give very strict discipline to their converts—they would permit no *oklehou*, no *hula*. And in their present-day dispensation, no polygamy, either. This I knew. "How comes it," I asked, "that you've made promises to four *wahine?*"

"One living in the valley. One dead. One in Hilo. One in Molokai."

Molokai! That sounded ominous—Molokai is the island on which is the leper settlement. Was this last *wahine* sick, I asked?

"Sick—Pake-sickness."

Island Days

Pake-sickness—Chinese sickness! That meant leprosy. I looked at the man; he sat on his horse in the rain, a childlike and pathetic smile on his face. But he brightened again. The *wahine* that lived with him now would do a *hula* for me if I came down with him into the valley. He had four horses, he added.

"How many men and women below?"

"Thirty *wahine*, thirty . . ."

"*Kanaka*," I said. He paused, not accepting the word. "Thirty *kane*," he said (*kanaka* means men, the native race; *kane* means husbands or heads of families).

"*Keiki* (children) too?"

"Plenty *keiki*," he intimated.

"The Pake—have they plenty?"

"Pake grow rice, not grow mans," he said. He invited me again to come down into the valley with him. But suddenly he started off and went down zigzag in the rain. He waved his hand to me as he went. For all his claim to being "*Kanaka pololei*," "straight Polynesian," there was much about him that reminded me of Connacht or Castile.

THE VILLAGE

The heavy surge of the ocean is pounding on the shore. The sky is all covered with shroud-like clouds. The little fields are green and they are marked off from each other by walls of loose stones. So much might remind me of a place in the West of Ireland. But the trees are stringy—a long piece of string with a knot on its top,

[47]

but kept upright and swaying—these are Pacific trees, the coconut palms, and they are everywhere around. The walls that mark off the fields seem to be made of black coals—they are of lumps of lava. I am on the island of Hawaii, and I am living in one of the few villages that the natives have kept for themselves.

The Hawaiians are the only Polynesian people who achieved a political organization that people of European stock had to take account of. That organization was the monarchy. At the time when Americans were making their Declaration of Independence, a king named Kamehameha was making himself master of this island, Hawaii. Subsequently, by force and diplomacy, he extended his power throughout the Eight Islands and left to his successors the Hawaiian monarchy. Kamehameha had the advice of that admirable sailor and explorer, Vancouver; he was aided, too, by the kidnapped sailors John Young and Isaac Davis; they helped him as boat-builders and artillery officers. But even with such aid and counsel the consolidation of power in the Hawaiian Islands was a remarkable military and political accomplishment—remarkable when we realize that the distance between one island and another is as great as the distance between England and France. Kamehameha was, as far as our knowledge goes, the greatest man the Polynesian race has produced. None of his successors were able men, but the great conqueror and law-maker was able to give prestige to a dynasty. Europeans and Americans coming to the islands found a court that they had to recognize. The monarchy in the islands, although the Kamehameha dynasty was broken, and although the *haole* or white interests made encroachments, remained a social fact; the king and queen, the Hawaiian notables at court, were socially very important people. Social prestige came to the Hawaiians through the court, and it is due to this former prestige that the Hawaiians of to-day have social consideration that English-speaking people so often deny to "natives." The crudest white people on the islands give the Hawaiians at least the same consideration they would give to Europeans of a different nationality. It is all the easier for them to do this because the colour-difference is slight and there is no difference in the physical make-up; it is self-evident that the Polynesians are more closely related to the Caucasians than they are to any other branch of the human family.

The Hawaiians did not have what the other Polynesian peoples had, an agricultural communism. The kings were absolute possessors of the soil of the islands, and the chiefs, the *alii*, held their lands from the kings. The common people rented their lands from the *alii*— in relation to the chiefs they were tenants at landlords' will; they paid for the use of the land in labor, farm-produce, pigs, dogs, and fish. If a tenant was too harshly treated he moved to the land of another *alii*. Wars and the succession of kings and chiefs with new division of land made for constant disturbance of tenants; the population was migratory within the islands, and the Hawaiian common people never acquired the attachment to particular localities and the devotion to the soil that European peoples have. Then, too, their family-life was and is very indistinct: there is no clear-cut word for "mother" or "father" in the language; *makua* means relation; add *wahine*, "woman" to it, or *kane*, meaning "male," and you have the words for "mother" and "father." The grandfather was as close to the child as the father, the grandmother as the mother; uncles and aunts were *makua* too. If children were scolded in their parents' houses, they went to an uncle's or an aunt's and stayed there; they had the right to dip in the *poi*-bowl. Children were always being adopted or given away—the custom still flourishes; there was no clear inheritance in land and there were no clear inheritors.

And there were no graves in Hawaii. A European might appeal to the graves of the fathers of the race and so awaken the devotion of the people for their soil. But the graves of their fathers and mothers were not there to attach Hawaiians to their locality. The dead were hidden in secret places: bones were needed for fish-hooks, and in a land where man was the largest-boned animal there was call for human bones. They were hidden lest the indignity of being used as fish-hooks or tools should befall them. And so, without attachment to a locality through land, through family, or through their fathers' graves, the Hawaiians did not become a peasantry in the European sense. In the middle of the nineteenth century, the king, by a renunciatory act, gave land with a secure tenure to the people. But now a growing plantation interest was in conflict with the

growth of peasant proprietorship in the islands; before
they were quite settled, the bulk of native tenants were
surrendering their water-rights to the plantation owners, and when the water-rights were given up, the taro
patches had to be abandoned. The Hawaiian culti-
vators—the real Kanaka people—have been pushed into
corners of the islands. And they are no longer pros-
perous fisherman; the Japanese with their power sam-
pans have gutted the fishing-grounds that the men of
the outrigger canoes were once lords of. The Hawaiians are now cowboys, boatmen, policemen, officials,
teachers, holders of political office. But still there are
men and women living off the taro patch; with these
we can share a life that is still distinctively Polynesian
in the islands.

The coconut palms near where I am are probably
the very trees that the first European mariners looked
on. On the beach are canoes with outriggers—that Polynesian device that made canoes uncapsizable. A man is
working in a garden with a primitive digging tool, the
wooden spade that was used when iron was a precious
metal in the islands; and in a shelter near by a blear-eyed
woman who looks at least a hundred years of age is
plaiting *lau-hala* fibre into a mat such as the first white
visitors to the islands slept on, while a boy with a stone
pestle in his hands is pounding *poi*. One could easily
imagine oneself a first-comer to this place. And yet, at
night, in the house we are very up-to-date. We sit around
a kerosene lamp—the Hawaiians are not quite used to
tables and chairs—and read the weekly journals; the

lamp is on the floor and we sit on mats. The journals are *Hoku o Hawaii*, "The Star of Hawaii," and *Nupepa Kuokuoa*, "The Independent Newspaper." Both have Hawaiian and foreign news with telegrams translated into Hawaiian from parts of the world where things are stirring. In the *Hoku o Hawaii* there is an instalment of a romance from a European language: I am trying to read "Leda Luigia," "Lady Luigia," which is a story of Rome in the time of Nero: I have begun to suspect that it is a translation of "Quo Vadis."

Like most Hawaiians, the people in whose house I am staying have ability in handicraft and decoration: all day the taciturn grandmother, seated on the floor, plaits a mat of *lau-hala*, long reed-like fibres softened in water, split, and then plaited as a child at home would plait a little mat of rushes; clean mats of the kind she is making cover the floors of the different rooms. And the bed-spread in the room I sleep in with its bold branching design of bread-fruit has been made in the house. All day the little girl—I must write her name carefully—Ka-puna-puke-lani (The Well at the Heavenly Gate) works with her needle. The different *lei* of ilima blossoms hung on the walls make a real decoration. They have no pictures; they have, as every Hawaiian household has, a row of photographs enlarged: the mild men and women who are the subjects look fearfully grim. I have come to think that Hawaiians do not look on photographs as we look on them, as pictured mementoes of friends and admired people: to them, I believe, a collection of photographs means a real society. Every

Island Days

Hawaiian has, or used to have, a *mele-inoa*, a name-song that would be known to him and his friends; I can believe that the Hawaiians in whose houses I have been often chant a brother's or sister's, a son's or a daughter's name-song under one of these photographs and have his or her presence there in a way that we could not have the presence of any of our friends.

Unlike the women of a European village, the women of this household have nothing to do with pigs or cattle. There are pigs here; they are turned out to the guava-jungles, and there, with their litters around them, they stay knocking the wild guava-fruit off the bushes and eating it where it lies on the ground: the guava that we know only when it comes to us as jelly. Like many other plants that were brought into the islands, the guava has spread until it has become a pest. There is no milking of cows in the mornings and evenings: we do without milk and butter here although there is plenty of pasture for cattle: the Hawaiians, in spite of the fact that cattle have been here since Vancouver's time, are not a milk- or butter-using people. I go with one of the boys to a cultivated field. Instead of ridges there are little mounds in the field—little mounds of black earth. In these mounds sweet potatoes grow. We grub them up and take a bagful for supper. Beside them is another vegetable—the small-leaved Chinese cabbage. These, too, we pull up, and cut some branches of bananas: the banana is the only fruit we can get; the Mediterranean fruit-fly has come in and has destroyed mango, pear, and orange.

A Half-Day's Ride or Estates in Corsica

I sit at a table and eat alone. In the next room the people of the house, seated on mats, eat in the Hawaiian fashion, a bowl of *poi* in the centre, with dishes of sweet potatoes, fish, and vegetables on the side. There is no difference in form or substance between breakfast, dinner, and supper. After supper we sit for a while on the verandah. Relations of the family come over from other houses and talk an Hawaiian that is full of barks and grunts. The boys and girls take out their ukelele or their steel guitars and play and sing Hawaiian melodies. I ask the little boy who has been playing the ukelele to tell me about the song he has just sung. "It's about a girl who runs away from her step-mother; she makes her work too hard and she gives her nothing to eat. She goes into the forest and lives on guavas and shrimps that she gets in the streams. There is an owl that helps her—I guess that owl is the ghost of her grandmother. One day the cowboys see her. They lasso her when she is in the stream." "Do they bring her back to her step-mother?" "No, they take her to their camp; I guess she stays with the boys." His mother, however, has a different ending for the song. The boys take her where there is a crowd and show her as a wild girl. The song is called "The Mountain Girl." Another is sung. This is about a woman going away—perhaps she is dying. She asks her husband to keep her diamond ring and wear it on his finger; she asks him to take care of her feather *lei* and not let the rain get on it; she asks him to wear her embroidered handkerchief round his neck and never to give it away to anyone.

Island Days

But I must not give the impression that I am in any sense at home here. I am as much at home as a canary would be in an ancestral forest. I discover now how dreadfully dependent we Westerners are on the formation we have imposed on our day: for us it must have a beginning, a middle, and an end. We have pleasantly marked the parts of it by breakfast, luncheon, and dinner, or by breakfast, dinner, and supper, and if these marks are not present we face tedium. My day, I have to confess, is filled with tedium. I get up and discover that there is no such thing as breakfast. There will be a meal when a sufficient number of people round me feel that they can't get on without eating something. That may be around three o'clock. Then there won't be anything as awakening as tea or coffee—there won't be milk even. When it is ready, I'll find that the meal is made up of biscuits from a store, pork, Chinese cabbage, sweet potatoes, and, of course, *poi*. I can get something to sip that is called Hawaiian tea; it is from the leaves of a plant that grows hereabouts, and it is served without milk or sugar. The first few sips make me feel that it is a good enough substitute for tea, but I am never able to finish the cup. Having finished this meal I contemplate a day in which there are no kindly divisions; I am appalled to find out how little prepared I am to do anything in such a day. I recall the atrocities mariners committed on being let loose here, and I feel sympathetic with the mariners. There are no fruits to pluck and eat as I wander through the lava-crossed terrain: the guava as fruit is singularly unrewarding, I find.

A Half-Day's Ride or Estates in Corsica

The language I hear spoken can never, I feel now, become part of my mentality. And I realize, as I note the look of isolation that the women have, that Gauguin is the only one who has rendered Polynesians. Yes, with their high-crowned, broad-brimmed hats of *lau-hala*, with their *lei* of flowers, the Hawaiian girls are striking —more striking than alluring, I think now. Their eyes tell their psychic history—dark, unluminous eyes. Well may they sing, "When the *willi-willi* trees take blossom, then the shark-god seizes on his prey," for the shark is about as playful a conception of the god of love as they can reach to; they have summer, but no spring-time; childhood and maturity, but no youth; they are not like the roses that have bud as well as blossom, but like their own hibiscus flowers that have their full bloom in a single day. And to increase my sense of alienation I discover my host and hostess in unlovely if familiar rôles— those of grasping hostel-keepers. I paid the woman for my board and lodging. Then the man came to me and demanded payment. I assured him that I had paid already. The woman came and protested that I hadn't. I suppose she wanted to get a little for herself and had weakly secreted what I had given her. I don't know what was in her mind or what was in his mind. I had no right to pay a *wahine* anyway, he told me; he was the one who was to get the money. I handed the dollars out again. And having seen as good an exhibition of greed and deception as could have been put on in any European caravanserai, I went and ate sweet potatoes and Chinese cabbage.

Island Days

A day comes when, a Ford car being available, we are able to make an excursion to a place that the family as well as myself want to go to. Ka-puna-puke-lani comes too. She brings her needle and a heap of carnations with her; all the way she is engaged in making *lei*. And so when her girl-friends come to meet her, our little Puna has beautiful wreaths to bestow on them. I take leave of the family and go exploring.

I come to where there is a *haiau*—a precinct for pagan sacrifices: it is an oblong mound of black stones with holes where the idols stood and with an enclosure where human beings were sacrificed. The coconut palms near it are probably the very trees that Captain Cook and his sailors looked on. And I come on habitations that are representative of the old Polynesian life: two grass-huts of the type that all the islanders lived in when Cook and Vancouver and the missionaries came. There are signs of life about one of them—nets for fishing and a few implements. It is a single-roomed house with the entrance at the gable-end; it was made of poles and rods lashed together by fibres, with long-stalked grasses woven through, grasses that now have become drab-coloured; *lau-hala* leaves and sugar-cane stalks formed the thatch. I have to enter crouching; within I can barely stand upright. Indeed, for us to live in an Hawaiian grass-hut would be like living in a hamper. The light comes through the open door. There is a raised place where the people lay on their mats; they kept

[57]

their belongings in calabashes hung from rods that went
lengthwise across the walls; these calabashes were carved
out of wood or made from the shell of a gourd; sometimes there was a calabash big enough to put a baby into.

That fine old Hawaiian antiquarian, David Malo
(his "Hawaiian Antiquities" does for the Hawaiian
past what O'Curry's "Manuscript Materials for Irish
History" does for the Irish past) has a chapter on the
building of the house. He begins with delightful na-
iveté. "The house," he says, "was the most important
means of securing the well-being of husband, wife, and
children, as well as of their friends and guests." Then
he goes on, "It was useful as a shelter from rain and
cold, from sun and scorching heat. Shiftless people oft-
times lived in unsuitable houses, claiming that they answered well enough. Caves, holes in the ground, and
overhanging cliffs were also used as dwelling-places by
some folk, or the hollow of a tree, or a booth. Some
people again sponged on those who had houses. Such
were called *o-kea-pili-mai* (sand that collects about a
thing), or *una-pehi-iole* (stone to throw at a rat). These
were names of reproach. But that was not the way in
which people of respectability lived. They put up houses
of their own." And then he describes how people built
such grass-huts as the one I am in, from the journey to
the mountain-side for the cutting of the timbers to the
trimming of the thatch over the door when the con-
secrating chant was made—

Severed is the piko of the house, the thatch that sheds the rain,
that wards off the evil influences of the heavens,

Island Days

The water-spout of Haakula-manu, Oh!
Cut now!
Cut the piko of your house, O Mauli-ola!
That the house-dweller may prosper,
That the guest who enters it may have health,
That the lord of the land may have health,
That the chiefs may have long life.
Grant these blessings to your house, O Mauli-ola,
To live till one crawls hunched up, till one becomes blear-eyed,
Till one lies on the mat, till one has to be carried about in a net.

There were people who built their houses and entered
them without any ceremony. They were of no account
in David Malo's estimation. "Such folk only cared for
a little shanty anyway; the fire-place was close to their
head, and the *poi*-dish conveniently at hand; and so,
with but one house, they made shift to get along." In
the grass-hut I was in, the fire-place was not close to
the head. Outside there was a little pit with stone around
it; the glowing charcoal was put in and the cooking was
done here. Beside the little pit I saw an iron kettle and
a smoothing iron. In the old days there was the oven—
emu—common to the whole village, in which pig, fish
wrapped in *ti*-leaves, bananas, taro, and yams were put
upon hot stones and covered with earth and cooked magnificently. I said common to the whole village, but I
should observe that in old Hawaii men and women ate
different food cooked in different ovens. They had to eat
in different places too. Hence the people who "with but
one house . . . made shift to get along," made a breach
in the conventions.

The other grass-hut, likewise deserted, is roomier;

thick stalks of sugar-cane are on the inside; outside, it is covered with long *pili*-grass. Until quite lately this hut was lived in by an old man. Often in the islands one comes across such forsaken houses—an old man is living by himself or a couple of old men are living together; they die, and the houses are left deserted. Well, the old man who lived here has only recently departed; near his door are growing the big leaves of the tobacco-plant that until lately had given him his smokes, and inside the house are his nets and his pipe. Going through things that were upon the floor I found some articles that were worth while as souvenirs—a *poi*-pounder shaped like an old pestle, a round black stone that was evidently used in a game like rounders, and, lastly, an ancient *ku-kui*. This I was delighted to find. It is the Polynesian lamp. I say lamp, but it is simply a hollow stone into which the oil from the *ku-kui* nut was pressed; the oil burned in a flare or it had a piece of tapa for wick. Simple as it is, it holds my imagination. By the light of such primitive lamps, stories were told, riddles were listened to, string-games or cats' cradles were made, in grass-huts such as this, century after century, on the islands from Tahiti to Hawaii.

STORY-TELLING

If ever you go to the islands and want to know the Hawaiians of the villages—the Kanaka of the taro patch—you can do no better than make friends with some of the Mormon missionaries and get one of the

Island Days

elders to take you around. I had read about Mormons in the pages of Robert Louis Stevenson and Conan Doyle, and I thought of them as bearded and over-bearing men of God. Well, the Mormon missionaries on the Hawaiian Islands are not of that mould. They are beardless, to begin with, and they are unassuming. These "elders" are, with few exceptions, all in their twenties—young men interrupting their college courses to give three years to mission work in the islands. And Salt Lake City does well in sending out men so young as these—youthful ardour and enthusiasm are tapped; the youthful dream of re-creating the world over-night goes to make these elders very earnest and very whole-hearted missionaries. They do not merit the reproach that was levelled at missionaries of another day, for they have literally no possessions. A concert or something of the kind is given for a benefit for one of them; he starts from Utah having bought his outfit with the money realized. Afterwards the missionary lives on money that relatives and friends send him. In every outlying part of the is-lands there is an elder or a group of elders visiting, ad-vising, and exhorting the scattered Hawaiians. They are all busy, they are all austere, they are all penniless; one, perhaps, will have a battered Ford to travel about in, but most of them make their calls as simple pedes-trians. They know the language; they have the entry into every simple Hawaiian home; they are respected by everyone for their probity and hard work. Well, one had arranged to meet me here, and he had been good enough to promise to take me further afield.

A Half-Day's Ride or Estates in Corsica

I wanted to have some of the stories that I had been making myself familiar with—the stories in the Fornander collection published by the Museum in Honolulu—brought to me in their real medium, the voice of the man or woman to whom they had been told, and who knew how to deliver them in the traditional way; I wanted to hear the story on the lips of the living storyteller so that I might get to know something of the intonation and gesture that went with it. I had been studying Hawaiian for a few months; I knew a little, but I could not hope to follow a story. The elder was going to interpret for me.

I went where there was a woman who had been with the professional entertainers at the court forty years ago. She had an English name now and was married to an English artisan. But, as I noted when I was presented to her, she was distinctly of the Polynesian aristocratic type—not the type that is large and imposing, but an unusually delicate type. She had been at King Kalakaua's court, and there were people who said she had royal blood in her.

Thirty years ago, she said, she could have told me Hawaiian stories of the old time. Now she had forgotten the very language in which she had told them and in which she had heard them told. For the stories that she had repeated were not in the common language. I understood what she meant, for it had become evident to me that the stories in the Fornander collection were not folk tales, but court romances; they would not, then, be in the idiom of the *kanaka*—the common people—

but in the idiom of the *alii*—the chiefs. The old gentle-woman would ponder over her memories, begin a story, tell a few lines, and then give up. But although I heard no story from her, I learnt much by being her auditor, by listening to her starts and watching her gestures. What wonderful gestures those delicate hands of hers made! They took me to the court, they made me understand something of the refinement that marked the difference between the entertainments of the court and those of the general people. Hers was an art for a fastidious audience.

From this we went to a house that was as near to squalor as an Hawaiian house can be—but of course no Polynesian home can have the dismalness and unclean-ness of our squalid places. An old woman was weaving —or rather plaiting—a *lau-hala* mat; after the elder had greeted her, she came to us and took us to the *lanai*, or verandah. I heard myself being spoken of as a *keiki haole*—a foreign child—who wanted to hear Hawaiian stories of the old time. She sat down on a mat and at once began the telling of a story.

This wild old woman had some wild youngsters in her train. I make special note about the wildness of these youngsters—her grandchildren, likely—because in Hawaiian houses the children are generally decorous. Perhaps I ought to attach wildness only to one of them, a girl of six who was noticeably dark for an Hawaiian. I think I heard them refer to this child as *polo-polo*, that is belonging to the South Seas; her father or mother might have been a Tahitian or Samoan. She did not at-

tend to the story that the old woman was telling; she
attended to me. She flung herself upon me. Not only
did she clasp and scratch and squeeze me; she bit me.
And she seemed to enjoy biting me, for she bit me again.
With difficulty I kept myself in a mood proper to an
audience. The old woman went right into the story;
she told it as a child might tell it, eagerly and laughingly.
I watched her gestures; they had less grace than the
gestures of the other woman, but they had expressive-
ness. I wondered at the flexibility of her wrists that
seemed to turn right around. No people are greater
masters of gesture than the Hawaiians; their faces and
their hands talk. As natural ballet-performers they must
be reckoned as before every other people. How wonderful their classical *hula* must have been, the *hula* performed by three hundred carefully trained players
which related some sacred story! A school should have
been established to keep the great *hula*—not the de-
graded *hula* that we can see now—in being.

I tried to keep the little *polo-polo* maiden at arm's
length while I watched and listened. The Mormon elder
listened, austerely translating sentence after sentence.
But there came a sentence that he wouldn't translate—
a sentence that made him blush. The old woman went
right on, not knowing that the Polynesian literalism that
she had given utterance to could cause the *haole* any
embarrassment; to her it was but a figure of speech; to
people of our speech it might appear a startling in-
decency.

Another interior: it is in a frame-house, but the people

are seated on the floor as they would have been in one of the grass-huts of the old days. A tub of *poi* is in the centre. Fingers are dipped in, entwined in the paste, and brought to the mouth. A whole family—it includes grandmothers, grandaunts, grandfathers, uncles, and all degrees of kindred—are seated around the tub. It is not only *poi* that is being eaten; I count nine smaller dishes around the *poi*-tub—sea-moss, raw fish, shell-fish, onions, and, as I guess, the flesh or the suckers of the loathly squid or devil-fish. I dip my fingers in the heliotrope-colored mass—the taro root baked and pounded—draw two fingers out, entangled in the paste, and eat. The *poi* has a sourish taste, like a dish made with sour milk. It would be bettered, I know, by the taste of raw fish. But I am afraid I might pick up a bit of squid.

In this old-world Polynesian group I sense the charm that the race possesses—the charm that appealed to Herman Melville and to Pierre Loti—a natural charm that is as much a gift as is the gift of beauty or the gift of artistic achievement. These old men and women, these young girls, seated around the *poi*-tub, are not claimant in any way; they are self-controlled and self-content. Their eyes rest upon us without any calcula-tion. Everything about them is genial; they laugh freely and easily. The old men and old women have faces that seem carved out of some dark-red wood; one of the old men has lines on his face that are like lines tattooed. The girls are soft of flesh, soft of curve, soft of smile; their dark hair falls loosely over their shoulders; their eyes are the Polynesian eyes, full and dark and un-luminous. One girl is golden brown; the other is quite dark. *"Aloha,"* they say, making long drawn the word that throughout all Polynesia means "love," "wel-come," "farewell." *"Ah-lo-ha," "aloha nui,"* we re-spond. These people have what none of the Hawaiians lack—a self-possession, a freedom from embarrassment that in Europe belongs only to the aristocracy.

HAWAIIAN POETRY

I go into many houses; in all of them I am received, not only graciously, but eagerly. I have become a sort of personage hereabouts: I am *haku-mele-mai-Ilani*, the poet from Ireland who has come to learn about the an-cient things of Hawaii. In clean houses, decorated with *lei* of artificial ilima flowers, dignified and scholarly-seeming old men, whole or part Hawaiians, recite for myself and the more knowledgeable friend who is with me. Poem after poem is repeated for us; my friend writes them down until he is weary of writing them. Many are *mele-inoa*—name-chants—poems made on the birth of a person and sacred to that person, curious rather than poetical, very obscure, not to say cryptic. The *mele-inoa* is a real poetic form; it might be in-troduced into European literature; in our languages it would have to be light and graceful, the verse of compli-ment or eulogy. I remember in looking over the verses written to a friend of mine, an Hawaiian lady, coming on a *mele-inoa* that was very delightful. It was in praise of my friend, who, amongst other names, has one that, translated, means "Standing Heavens." The event that had given her this name was alluded to, words were introduced that suggested the heavens so that, if we were quick-witted, we could guess the name before it was announced, and then, for the last line, "Standing Heavens, claim your song." It would be difficult, I suppose, to make *mele-inoa* in lands where genealogy is not considered, and where personal names have not the concrete meaning that they have among the Polynesians. Besides such *mele* we were given many *mele* about places; each island has its *mele;* so has every little valley, river, and village—*mele* that weave the places into a tradition going back to Wakea and Papa, the mythical ancestors of the people and the islands.

Hawaiian poetry—and this is probably true of Polynesian poetry generally—comes from a root that is different from the root that our poetry comes from. In our poetry the primary intention is to communicate some personal emotion; in their poetry the primary intention, I believe, is to make an incantation, to cast a spell. Hear Hawaiian *mele* chanted with all of their prolonged vowel sounds, and you will be made to feel that what is behind the *mele* is not a poet, but a magician. I can think of only one or two poems in English that are in their intention, in their evocative sound, anything like Hawaiian *mele*. One is the incantation that "A. E." has put into his "Deirdre," the incantation that bespells Naisi and his brothers. In the play, as it was first given,

A Half-Day's Ride or Estates in Corsica

"A. E." himself used to chant the spell with the very intonation, as I now discover, of the surviving Hawaiian chanters—

> Let thy Faed Fia fall,
> Mananaun MacLir.
> Take back the day
> Amid days unremembered.
> Over the warring mind
> Let the Faed Fia fall,
> Mananaun MacLir;
>
> Let thy waves rise,
> Mananaun MacLir,
> Let the earth fail
> Beneath their feet,
> Let thy waves flow over them,
> Mananaun—
> Lord of Ocean!

The open Polynesian syllables, with their vowels arbitrarily lingered on, naturally give more of the effect of an incantation than even the lines that have sounds as evocative as "Mananaun, Lord of Ocean." Another poem that I can imagine being chanted in the Hawaiian way, and producing the same effect of incantation, is Blake's—

> Hear the voice of the Bard,
> Who present, past, and future sees,
>   Whose ears have heard
>   The Holy Word
> That walked among the ancient trees!

Island Days

Calling the lapsed soul,
And weeping in the evening dew,
   That might control
   The starry pole,
And fallen, fallen light renew!

But if Hawaiian poetry had in it only this evocative sound it would be of little interest to us who have been trained to appreciate different qualities in poetry. It has a personal and human appeal, too. And the Hawaiian poet has anticipated effects that the cultivated poets of our tradition have been striving for: he is, for instance, more esoteric than Mallarmé and more imagistic than Amy Lowell.

Every Hawaiian poem has at least four meanings: (1) the ostensible meaning of the words; (2) a vulgar double meaning; (3) a mythological-historical-topographical import; and (4) the *mauna*, or deeply hidden essential meaning. I have sat gasping while, in a poem of twelve or twenty lines, meaning under meaning was revealed to me by a scholar who knew something of the Hawaiian tradition.

But the main thing that Hawaiian poetry has to offer an outsider is the clear and flashing images that it is in its power to produce. The Polynesian language, it should be noted first, has no abstract terms. If an Hawaiian wants to refer to my ignorance he speaks of me as having the entrails of night; if he wants to speak of someone's blindness he will speak of eyes of night. Abstractions become images in the Polynesian language. And the people themselves have an extraordinary sense of the visible things in their world: they have, for instance, a dozen words to describe the shades of difference in the sea as it spreads between them and the horizon. Their language forces them to an imagistic expression. Their poetry, then, when it is at all descriptive, is full of clear and definite images. I open Nathaniel Emerson's "Unwritten Literature of Hawaii," a book upon the *hula* which is at the same time a complete anthology of Hawaiian poetry, and I find—

Heaven-magic, fetch a Hilo pour from heaven!
Morn's cloud-buds, look! they swell in the East.
The rain-cloud parts, Hilo is deluged with rain,
The Hilo of King Hana-kahi.

Surf breaks, stirs the mire of Pii-lani;
The bones of Hilo are broken
By the blows of the rain.
Ghostly the rain-scud of Hilo in heaven.

The cloud-forms of Pua-lani grow and thicken.
The rain-priest bestirs himself now to go forth,
Forth to observe the stab and thrust of the rain,
The rain that clings to the roofs of Hilo.

I know one poem in English that in its clear and flashing imagery resembles the passages that we must regard as the best of Hawaiian poetry: that poem is Meredith's "Nuptials of Attila." No Hawaiian poet has been able to tell a story, no Hawaiian poet has been able to give an organization to a poem that is at all like Meredith's, but all this is like Hawaiian poetry—

Island Days

Flat as to an eagle's eye
Earth hung under Attila.

. . . . .

On his people stood a frost.
Like a charger cut in stone,
Rearing stiff, the warrior host
Which had life from him alone,
Craved the trumpet's eager note
As the bridled earth the Spring.

"THE ISLAND OF THE HEAVENLY ROSE"

I am writing this on another island—the island of
Maui—"Maui moku loke lani." Each island has, in
addition to its geographical name, a name derived from
its *lei*—that is from the wreath of flowers that is distinctively its own. The rose is the flower of this island,
and so Maui becomes (remember that every vowel is
pronounced) "Moku loke lani"—"island of the heavenly (or royal) rose." The rose was brought into the
islands as you can see if you compare the word *loke* with
the word "rose"—our "r" becomes an "l" and our "s"
(along with several other consonants) becomes a "k."
Well, the depredations of some beetle or another have
all but destroyed roses on the other islands. They still
flourish here, however; I see roses of the white and red.
The lily flourishes, too; there are red lilies everywhere,
and the white lily is even more queenly here than in other
places. And over the walls of the gardens the bougainvillæa comes in a cascade of blossom (why, by the way,
do men impose their names upon flowers? Monsieur de

A Half-Day's Ride or Estates in Corsica

Bougainville left his name on an island, and he should have been content with perpetuating it that way; as a name for a flower it is prosaic and a misfit). What a riot of blossoms, one says, when one looks on the bougainvillæa for the first time. "No, I am not a child of riot and extravagance," it might, however, answer. "Look at me and note what little luxury I have come out of." It simply joins four leaves together, stains them magenta, or mauve, or maroon, and so has its blossom; working in this homely way it can well afford to be abundant.

The little houses here are of board; they all have a *lanai* on their front. Beside the houses are banana patches; they are about the size of the cabbage-gardens in front of farm-houses in Ireland or Scotland; the great leaves of the banana plant are like long green sails, and I can fancy their turning little mills. There are always a few papiaa trees before the houses. If ever a tree was an humble imitator it is the papiaa: it has modelled itself obviously on the coco-nut palm; it has the umbrella foliage and the cluster of fruit. But the imitation is infantile; there is no girth to its stem and it does not reach to half the height of the coco-nut palm.

Again the Pacific is below me. This time I am riding along the gulches that run down to it. Above us and below us are those strangely formed gulches; they are humped and hollowed out and are greatly verdurous. As if along a great spiral we keep mounting up; again and again we come to where the Pacific is below us. I see trees that are celebrated in Hawaiian tradition. That tree with the broad green leaves that look as if they were silvered over is the kukuli—the candle-nut tree. They grow in downward sweeps following the lines of the streams. I pull some of the nuts—the tree bears blossoms, young nuts and ripened nuts at the same time; the nuts are about the size of pigeons' eggs. I strip off the outer peel and find a nut that has the feeling of a piece of soap; within are two others: it was these inner nuts that gave light in the grass-houses of old Hawaii. Then there are lehua trees; its flower makes the *lei* that is for the warrior, the lover, and the king. This flower is not formed of petals but of scarlet threads bunched together like the down of a thistle.

Upward and onward. We hear the grunting of a boar in the underbrush, for there is wild pig here; we hear the pheasant's throaty crow. Wild pig is the domestic pig gone native; the pheasants were introduced from Formosa; they feed upon the lantana bush that was brought in from Mexico and that now has become a pest. Doves, generally in pairs, feed upon our path; they are turtle-doves that have been brought from China.

Our spiral turns again, and now we are descending. There is a beach beyond, and straggling from the beach is an Hawaiian village. To one used to the sight of a European village this does not look a village at all; no street goes by the houses; no smoke rises up in the clear air; there is no lowing of cattle. We hear cocks crowing, however, as we ride down through the mist. And there are goats; they crop along the path that we follow. Down by the beach birds are flying; their cry brings back the memory of storm-swept Atlantic beaches. They are plover, the kolea of the Hawaiians. Like the Irish poets, the Hawaiians make good use of the kolea—*O ka hua o ke kolea, aia i Kahiki*—"The plover's egg is laid in Kahiki," that is, in another world. In that line the Hawaiian poet emblems the mystery of love that comes as the plover comes, mysteriously across the sea. Then through the mist comes a dear and familiar bird's song. Yes, the sky-lark is indeed singing by these Pacific pastures; it has been brought here from New Zealand, the sky-lark of home, acclimatized to certain of the Pacific islands. I think of Synge's poem—

> Friend of Fletcher, Shelley, Beaumont,
> Lark of Ulster, Meath, and Thomond,
> Heard from Smyrna and Sahara
> To the surf of Connemara,
> Bird of April, June, and May,
> Sing loudly this, my Lady Day.

Mountain-Dwellers

Maui, the island, is dominated by Hale-a-ka-la, "The House of the Sun," a mountain that must have been the greatest volcano that the earth in its present form has known. Its crater, above the clouds, is twenty miles across. Hale-a-ka-la is a proper setting for the greatest exploit in Polynesian tradition: on the top of this mountain Maui the demigod snared the sun; he had been going too swiftly across the heavens; Maui held him until he promised to slacken his pace; since that time men and women have been able to do twelve hours' work in a day.

I am glad to have the chance of going part way up this great mountain. On the side of it, three thousand feet up, there lives a Portuguese woman that a friend of mine wants to visit. Our way is by fields of sugar-cane, hundreds of acres of the cane that is greener than any other crop that grows. Then there are cacti. They have been brought in to give green food to ranch cattle; as I look on them, I think that cacti growing above the green fields of sugar-cane are as extraordinary a sight as any I am likely to see: there is something militant in their dark-green formation: it is as if the cacti were on a march down the hill; within the queer branches one imagines warriors in Aztec masks; the trees crouch together; they embrace like alligators standing on their tails; out of their twisted branches come geometrical, futuristic pods—it is these that the cattle eat.

There is no winter here; you put down a crop as you take one up; all the year round crops are coming out of the ground. Any vagrom man could squat in some out-of-the-way place here and put up a few boards that would give him a shelter. He could kill wild pig and pheasant—wild turkey even. Coming back from his shooting, he could gather coffee-berries and fill his bag with wild bananas. He could have his tobacco growing beside his door. He could fish in the streams and the sea. But if he went to stay in a hotel on the island everything to eat would be frozen or in a tin; his mutton would be from New Zealand; his butter and as-

paragus would be from California; he would have con-
densed milk; he would have fish that certainly did
not come out of home waters. How badly, indeed, do
we manage things in our civilization!

We go up the hill towards the homestead. No sugar-
cane can grow here, and so the planters have left the
land to homesteaders. "It is a very old place," the
Portuguese woman who is with us keeps telling us. "The
house was built thirty years ago." There is young corn
in the field, onions, too, and cabbages. The house is of
boards; it is whitewashed and European-seeming.
Outside, geraniums are growing in bushes; there are
fuchsias, too; then there are spearmint and herbs that
are used in medicine or in cookery. It is a European
peasant's house on the side of this mountain of the
Pacific.

My friend wants to take Lisa as a maid. She is with
us to get her mother's permission to go, or rather, to stay
in the town below. Manoel, her young brother, and
Isabella, her younger sister, come to meet her. The
grave-faced mother takes us within; she speaks English
with difficulty, having come to the islands when she was
too grown up to go to the schools in the place. So her
sister-in-law explains.

Here is the Virgin and Child: before the shrine the
wonderful white lilies that grow on the mountain-side
have been placed. With her veil across her head the
Portuguese mother sits in the room where the shrine is,
taking this and that into consideration. Lisa's aunt rec-
ommends that she be given permission to stay below.

Island Days

Lisa puts in a word in Portuguese as she looks at her wrist-watch. At last it is settled; Lisa is given permission to stay with my friends.

Her aunt tells me that Portuguese girls always give their earnings to their mothers. Then, when it comes to marriage, the mother provides the girl with trunks of linen and the like. "So much they give to their daughters," the aunt said. Then she began lamenting that the Portuguese girls did not always marry Portuguese men —they married Filipinos and all sorts of people—Japanese even. She did not mind their marrying Americans —but Filipinos! The Filipinos, I thought, have quite a way with the girls of the islands: a little while before, I had been talking with an Hawaiian who got into a most un-Hawaiian temper over the fact that Hawaiian girls were marrying into that stock. "The worst people that ever came into the islands," he asserted. And now the Portuguese woman was denouncing their pretensions to the daughters of her people. They called themselves Catholics, she went on, but she could assure me that with the Filipinos, Catholicism went a very little way.

Lisa packed a basket; while we waited for her, her brother and sister went to the hillside to get lilies for us. Lisa is a broad-shouldered girl; she has black, bobbed hair and strongly marked down on her upper lip. She speaks Portuguese and English with some Japanese and Hawaiian that she learnt from girls in her school; so Lisa is quite a linguist. I thought how secure her people were. They were above the villages that were just "camps" for their occupiers, they were far away from the plantations with their long hours of drudgery; they had the peasant way of living that went back to a European tradition—the tradition that gave the elders such repose; I was thinking what advantages Lisa had over the others—Filipinos, Chinese, Japanese, and other uprooted people. As I was thinking about this, Lisa came out with her basket, and Isabella came up with her arms filled with wonderful lilies. "You will be glad to come back to this place, I suppose," I said to Lisa. She laughed. "It's kind of nice," she said. Then she added, "It's very old up here—thirty years my mother is here." "It is like Europe," I remarked, for I was listening to the larks who were singing above on the mountain-side. "Is it?" asked Lisa. "But more lovely," I said, for Lisa was now standing beside a peach tree that was in bloom in March. "It's kind of slow," said Lisa, "old Portuguese style, you know. They're not with the times," said Lisa. She lifted up her basket and went joyfully towards the car that would bring her away from the homestead. Her stately mother, the veil across her head, stood at the door of the little house; the grave Isabella and the quiet Manoel, having given us their offering of lilies, went back.

And so to the metropolis of the island. There are moving-picture houses there—two of them; there are shops, Japanese and American; there are two hotels in which overseers, teachers, travelling salesmen stay. There are people moving in the street, different human beings to rub up against and to talk to. Yes, indeed, it might be very stirring to live down there. And from

Island Days

the port, a boat goes twice a week, taking people over
to Honolulu, a night's journey away.

THE ECONOMIC FOREGROUND

Flames are twisting, crackling, rising—a whole field
of flame. The field is being fired to get rid of the
growth of leaves so that the sugar-cane be more easily
cut. The burning field makes a spectacle to wonder at,
for the cane-field is a jungle that is hard to break
through. And that being so, a remarkable technique is
needed to prevent a conflagration that might sweep
through hundreds of acres. There are firebreaks, of
course, and the burning is done at a time when the wind
may not sweep the fire through acres of cane. It is very
early in the morning when I look upon this field of burning cane. From the steamer I had seen a red patch on a
hill far away. It had looked to me like an active volcano.
And then I had heard someone say that it was cane being
burned.

The board-houses by the roadway are for the workers
in the plantations: there is light in the houses still—
a hanging bulb of electric light. Japanese women are
stirring about; their husbands are already in the cane-
fields. I meet a child now and again on the roadway although there is a large star still in the sky. The island
of the cane-fields is surely a land of early risers.

In acres and hundreds of acres spreads the green that
is richest of all greens—the green of the sugar-cane. It
is only when we get away from where water can be

poured out, it is only when we go up the mountains or get to places where a black lava-crust lies upon the earth, that we lose sight of that triumphant green. Sooner or later, if we would understand the life of these islands, we shall have to go by one of the roads that lead through this green growth and come to someone who can tell us about the plantations.

Practically everything that comes to the islands is in exchange for sugar or pineapple. And sugar is the main, the staple interest. Of the islands, as distinct from the islets in the group, all, except Molokai which is lacking in water, have great sugar-plantations—Oahu, Kioui, Maui, Hawaii. But it is on the island of Hawaii that the production of sugar is at its simplest; there the abundance of water permits of direct transportation from the field to the factory and furnishes power besides for the running of the factory. Here bundles of cut cane are rushed through flumes to the factory. This is a flume; bundles of cane are being swept along in it; day and night, in a twenty-four-hour shift, this flume and the flumes that converge on it are carrying the cane from the field into the factory—carrying it right into the machinery that cuts it, crushes it, and makes it yield up its juice. The heavy rainfall on this island makes this direct transportation possible; on the other islands there is only water for irrigation purposes.

The conversion of land and labor into wealth by way of the cane-plantation and the sugar-factory has a rather terrifying simplicity here. There is no curve in the conversion; it is in a perfectly straight line. The islands have concentrated practically the whole of their economic life on the production of sugar. There are pineapples. But the cultivation of pineapples, although a deal of land and labor go to it and although there are great returns from it, is still in the experimental stage as compared with cane.

The man I am with is the overseer of the greatest plantation on the islands. He looks like a leader of men besides. I saw him leaping a wall of flame like Sigurd, leading his men to the control of a fire that had swept through the brakes. He speaks to the gangs we meet in Hawaiian, Spanish, and pidgin-English. His is an eleven-hour working-day; he is on the field from five o'clock in the morning until four in the afternoon, directing the men and working with them.

He knows everything about cane, from the seed to the crystals. Probably no crop in the world is so closely regarded by experts as the cane that flourishes in these Pacific islands. As I go along I ask about figures noted on boards. They refer to special varieties planted here, varieties that are being observed. If a variety shows signs of degenerating, the expert finds new seeds or brings in some lucky "sport" to take its place. In this plantation they are watching a small black cane that has been produced in one of the South Sea islands: they expect that this variety will be more productive or more disease-resisting than any cane that has been cultivated hitherto.

The field never lies fallow: put back some nitrates into the soil and a crop can be taken out of it year after year. A crop is always there. As I go through the plantation I note three stages in the continuous crop-production. There is a field that the power-cultivator has broken: bundles of cut cane lie near to be planted in ridges by the women and children of the plantation. Here are fields where the crop is due to ripen in six, nine, or twelve months. Here are fields that have been burned and are now being cut.

Sigurd tells me that for him there is no more magnificent prospect than these green expanses and high jungles of cane. He knows them in every shade and in every stage. For eleven months he rejoices in the sight of the cane; then he gets tired and he must have a month away from it; he goes to Honolulu, visits, dances, plays, sits in the Pacific Club. I wonder what he can get out of this strenuous and devoted service. A good salary, no doubt. But his great reward is in accomplishment—in this co-ordination of effort, in his vision of these expanses ever green and ever productive, in the swiftness and effectiveness of the factory. This, no doubt, is adequate reward. I wonder what the men coming along in gangs, the men to whom he speaks in Hawaiian, Spanish, and pidgin-English, feel they get out of it—these Kanakas, Filipinos, Portuguese, Porto Ricans, Japanese, Koreans.

We follow the flume that is sweeping to the factory the brown bundles of cane. We come to the mill and are ready to view the climax of all this drama of growth and labor. There are not many hands about. As the cane comes down it is cut by four knives that are at the factory entrance; it is carried a little lower down and crushed; I see the oozing juice.

I follow it as the juice is drawn to compartments upstairs; there are great enclosed boilers with glass retorts on the outside which permit one to see the dark-brown juice as it becomes more and more purified. Molasses is formed; by centrifugal force the sugar is separated, and the molasses again is made to yield up its sugar. Brown sugar comes out warm; we see it packed into bags and stowed away in the wagons that will take it to the steamer; in New York it will be refined into the sugar that we use. The bundle of cane that I saw being rushed along by the flume has added its crystallized juices to the mass that has gone into one of these bags.

There is a laboratory and counting-house in the mill. In the counting-house the manifest of the produce of plantation and mill is looked at: sixteen thousand bags of sugar to-day; a hundred and ten tons.

Since I have been in the islands I have heard the word "camp" over and over again. Now although one-tenth of the military forces of the American Republic is stationed in these mid-Pacific islands, the "camps" spoken of are not for soldiers; they are for laborers, for the workers in the plantations. For the Hawaiian Islands are singular in this—whereas other countries have not always enough work for their populations, these islands have not population enough for their work. Since the Thirties and Forties when the monarchy sanctioned the importation of Chinese, labor agents have been searching for and bringing into the islands labor from many quarters—Chinese, Portuguese, Japanese, Filipino, Porto Rican, Korean. I come to note the different types as I go through the plantation. The Japanese have the biggest quota, the Portuguese come next, then the Filipinos. Few Hawaiians are on the plantations; the Kanaka, a small farmer and fisherman by tradition, does not take to the impersonal, hard-driven labor of the cane-fields.

The very word "camp" gives the history and status of this imported labor. There are no villages here for the plantation workers, for villages belong to generations of people, and these men and women have not grown up, they have been dumped down, on this land. The word "camp," too, implies something regulated, and the places where the workers and their families live are under supervision.

And yet the collections of houses that form the newer "camps," from the point of view of hygiene or of comfort, are ahead of most villages in Europe. They are neat, these frame-houses; they have a wash-house for the family outside with a shower-bath, and every "camp" has a club-house for men. The schools that are about the plantations are pleasanter than any schools I have been in elsewhere; the teachers are of a good type, and they have not only consideration but affection for their polyglot charges. The people who live on the plantations have wages that would look good to a farmer in many parts of America. They have a dollar a day to begin with. They have a bonus with this pay. They have money for overtime, and their women and children are able to work alongside if they like and make a good addition to the wage of the head of the family. They have a free house; they have free light, fuel, nursing, and medical attendance. The plantation owners are quite open to suggestions for the betterment of life in the "camps"; indeed they have, in several places, brought in enlightened and devoted welfare workers who are putting into operation programmes for social betterment.

And yet, if there is one thing clear about it all, it is that in this beautiful country, in this ideal climate, in this paradise for children, the workers, with steady jobs and many advantages, are not at all anxious to stay on the plantations. Few of the children grown up here go into the cane-fields. The adult workers do not regard themselves as settled here; when they can, they pull up stakes and leave the islands. I have an idea that to a great extent the aversion to the plantation begins in the "camp." It might be wise for the plantation-owners to discard the word with its suggestion of transitoriness and regulation and rootlessness. These collections of houses should be given names. The namelessness of the place he lives in is one more way of showing the worker that, for the plantation-owner, he is only the economic man.

In the "camps" there is no wine-drinking, no cock-fighting, no uproarious love-making, no festivities that go on through days and nights; a man cannot have a good row with his wife, a family cannot throw things at one another without a camp-policeman appearing on the scene. There is nothing, in short, to remind one of the normal, dramatized life of the European village. There are movies that the plantation worker and his family can go to; the young people of the "camps," no doubt, have ways of getting together, but human life is certainly subdued—it is subdued to produce the economic person, the man or woman who can put in eleven good hours in plantation work.

There is something in human nature that will not have it that man is just an economic creature. He is an economic creature some of the time, but most of the time man is something quite different. "Sometimes we experience surprise that they should labor so arduously at their sport and so leisurely at their plantations and houses, which, in our opinion, would be far more conducive of their advantage and comfort." So wrote the Reverend Mr. Ellis, an early missionary, of the Hawaiians. "They generally answered that they built houses and cultivated their gardens from necessity, but followed their amusements because their hearts were fond of them." The Hawaiians who made that answer spoke on behalf of the whole human race—the Japanese in present-day Hawaii, perhaps, excepted. Man treated as an economic creature—even well treated as such—is left with much of a grievance. And here the unconscious and the conscious patterns of his life are made divergent.

They stand, these nameless villages, through all the greater Hawaiian islands, collections of board-houses without chimneys beside the green of the cane-fields and enclosed by the many-blossomed hibiscus hedges with their high greenery. The races are segregated; one does not find Japanese and Portuguese families, or Filipino and Porto Rican, living side by side. Near the camp is the plantation store with its enormous array of goods in cans, biscuits, and salt meats, with its display of camp-notices in Hawaiian, Japanese, Portuguese, Spanish, and the odd-looking Malay language full of "ngs" and "bangs" that a section of the Filipinos have for their vernacular. Down the road is the school charmingly arranged in bungalows, with trees and delightful flowers around and with children within and without—Japanese children mostly, with their shy geniality, their slit eyes and microscopic noses, and their little flowered kimonos—and with a few Hawaiians, some Portuguese, and other children representing odd racial mixtures. One is made sad to think that so few of these little people will grow up with any attachment to this beautiful place, that they will come to have the minds of transients, the children of the camp.

Out in the cane-fields the men and women are working, and the *luna* or overseer watches this group and that group. What do they feel about their work in the field and their life in the camp? They are not inarticulate, this alien-speeched folk, and one of their testaments has come my way. It is a poem that, for all its uncouth foreign words and all its cramped expression, has power and impressiveness—has indeed something of the directness of a poem written from some modernist formula. The appeal made is not to class interest but to something in the human spirit.

A Half-Day's Ride or Estates in Corsica

BATTLE HYMN OF THE LABORERS

by a laborer of Makaweli

At four-thirty the bugle sounds.
Still camps rouse into motion,
And the noise of men breaks the stillness of night.
Companies are armed—
Regiment of hapaiko men,
Regiment of "cut cane" men,
Regiment of hanawai,
Regiment of hoehana.

A mixed battalion of Japanese, Filipinos, Chinese,
Koreans, Portuguese, and Spanish.
Our Captain is mean.
He rides on a horse with a big rod.
Companies are divided in two;
They press forward riding on train,
To the Castle of the Capitalists,
To the Castle of the Poor.
Hapaiko! Cut cane!

Hey! Enemies are strong—
Big rain, terrible storm.
Why fear, you cowards!
Front-line men are killed,
Second-line men are wounded,
Third-line men are aged.
Alas! Only help is National Guard.
Hapaiko! Hanawai!

You're shot!
Your bayonet is broken!
Your ammunition is gone!

Island Days

You fool!
Fight! Fight until it falls—
Castle of the Poor!
Cut cane! Hoehana!

Fight!
Fight for the freedom of mankind!
Scholars, be baptized with mud!
Priests, be baptized with spirit!
Rich men, be baptized with love!
Poor men, be baptized with freedom!

Charge!
Charge!
Be not misled.
Hapaiko! Cut cane!
Hanawai! Hoehana!

There is no mistaking the resentment that is back of the poem. Written by a Japanese plantation laborer, it was published in a Japanese newspaper; it was brought to the notice of the Hawaiian attorney-general, who had to consider whether the publisher of the poem should be tried for revolutionary intent. Thanks to its being brought to the notice of the law and being published as a document in the case, we can glimpse plantation life as seen by an embittered plantation worker.

The "Captain" who is "mean," who "rides on a horse with a big rod" is the *luna* or overseer. The rod that is so sensationally noted is only a riding-crop. "Front-line men are killed"—that refers to the first importation of Japanese laborers who are now all dead or

incapacitated by age. "Second-line men are wounded."
That is an allusion to the crippling effect of the *hapaikou*
work, at which men weighing one hundred and forty
pounds or less pack bundles of cane weighing one hundred and eighty pounds or more from the fields to the
freight cars. "It is true that they themselves set the
weight of their own bundles," says the Honolulu journal that published the poem after it had been brought to
the attorney-general, "but it is also true that after five
or six years of it, they become permanently deformed
and can be distinguished from their fellows by the
depression of the shoulders on which the bundles have
rested. It should be said in justice that the planters
have for years been seeking to develop mechanical load-
ers that could compete in the field against the human
pack animal and that it appears they are on the verge
of success." The flume and the wires that carry the
bundles from the upland plantations to the factories are
mitigating the labor of the human pack animal.

> You're shot!
> Your bayonet is broken!
> Your ammunition is gone!

All this has reference to a strike and to the dissipation
of the strike-fund.

And now I feel that I am watching a game played by
invisible giants as I stand and watch the sacks of sugar
reach the hold of the steamer. A sack bowls down the
shoot; it bumps, strikes a heavy net, and plunges down
into the hold. I watch the throws, fascinated. An-

other sack comes along, strikes the net, rebounds, and piles itself upon sacks that have gone wide of the hold. They will be flung down by men on the steamer. And watching the game, or walking up and down near the steamer, are characteristic island groups.

There are dark-faced Hawaiian girls with *lei* of yellow ilima blossoms around the brim of their hats; there are Japanese women small and neat, with their obis in tucks behind; there are Filipino women with their full white dresses, loose jackets and their unshod feet— women broad but upstanding, oddly lithe, with something of the jungle still about them; they all carry babies, and dogs keep curiously near them; there are tall, dark-faced men, Hawaiians and part-Hawaiians, delegates to the Legislature who are going by steamer to Honolulu; they, too, have the *lei* of yellow ilima. All look on, and the invisible giants go flinging weights against the net. It is towards evening; there is sunlight upon everything, and there is a great segment of a rainbow in the sky.

A MARINE ADVENTURE

IN A city that fronts Bimini, the island on which
Ponce de Leon expected to find the Fountain, I entered
an aquarium, going through a hedge of blossoming ole-
anders. It was sunken, spacious, dim and cool. I looked
upon Mud Fish that persuaded us they were not fossils
by being not inert; long and dull-colored, they made
a shoal at the bottom of their tank. I looked upon Sun
Fish that made a shoal, but midway in the water, and
had a pulsating life in them. I saw fish in ones and twos
whose eyes had terrible intentness or else trouble, puzzle,
and loss. I looked upon Parrot Fish whose lovely blue
fades into crystal whiteness, and Angel Fish with their
iridescent colors. And I saw the Octopus with sunken
eye that looks like a mouth, and a mouth that looks like
a vent, and with crawling skin that can make him eye-
less and mouthless, a thing that is neither beast nor fish
and that is yet terribly at home in the clean element.
I liked the open blackguardism of the Sharks after I had
looked upon the Octopus. I saw them going about in
their depths, swaggering fellows. And I saw fish with
piercing blades in front of them and with blades that
were wavy like Malay krises. I looked down on shape-
less bulks that were a herd of Sea Cows. And then I
came on fish that were as terrifying as the Octopus, but
not in the same nightmare-like way.

A Marine Adventure

Out of a great shell three snake-like heads lifted themselves up, heads that swayed and mouths that gaped. I thought they should be named Medusa Fish, but they were named Moray. Like three heads upon one body they raised themselves out of the shell. And from a cleft in the coral another raised itself like a powerful, distended arm. Their strange uprightness, their patient, swaying motion made them seem other than fish. They had greenish color that made them not like things seen in the sea, but things seen in a cavern that Leonardo da Vinci might have painted. What deep-sea lives were they striving to fascinate as they lifted themselves out of the great shell or out of the cleft in the coral?

"Any information you'd like to have?" The young lady in charge of the watery exhibition spoke to me. She was closed in with pieces of coral and by those fan-shaped growths that may be coral or hardened sponges, by huge round sponges and great shells that had in them the colors of dawns and sunsets. She had been powdering her nose, or putting stick on her lips, or combing her hair since my entrance.

"The Sword-fish—are they dangerous?" I asked.

"Oh, yes," she said. "They very often slash another fish in two." Her glaucous eyes were full of appreciation of the feat. "I can watch them do it," she said. "And here's an interesting thing. One of our Cow-fish has had a baby Cow-fish."

"Really?" I remarked.

"Yes," she said. "She's nursing it now. A baby that weighs sixty pounds." Never had I seen such intense

A Half-Day's Ride or Estates in Corsica

sympathy for a Cow-fish as was in her eyes. "I can tell you about coral, sponges, sharks and Cow-fish," she went on.

"Aren't you changing the color of your lips?" I said.

"To geranium," said she. "I spend most of my time making up."

"It would be nice to see you outside," I ventured. "There is dancing on the beach. . . ."

"Oh, I never can dance," she cried, and the corals and sponges and shells did not permit my seeing her feet. "And I never keep appointments," she said.

"Of course not," I agreed. "And I am very lucky to be able to come on you here and have you talk to me."

"Any information I can give you?" she began.

"What songs the Sirens sang . . ." I murmured.

"What about them?" said she.

"None of us know what they were," I said. "You can tell me."

"No one ever asks me about them," she said.

"It has long been thought," I went on, "that they are not beyond all conjecture. But I want very much to hear what they were."

"Don't you know?" she asked.

"No. Tell me. The songs the Sirens sang—what were they?"

"They were the usual songs," she replied.

THE COUNTRY OF THE CRANES

A DUG-OUT canoe in which is an Indian fisher takes
me to a Seminole encampment. The huts in it are as
simple as can be: a platform of board with a thatch of
reed above it; here, on bare boards, families sleep at
night. They have racoons in cages, and, fenced in from
the canal, in ditched-in water, alligators; some are full-
grown and some are little lizards. But why do they
keep alligators? I learn that alligators take a long time
to grow up; people buy the little ones from the Indians
and keep them as odd pets.

On the platforms, under the reed-thatch, girls are
seated like tailors, turning handles of sewing-machines,
cutting up various stuffs and stitching them across. So
they get the very varied colors and designs that I see
in the women's dresses.

They wear capes of puce or purple coming over skirts
that are pleated and flounced and that go down to their
naked feet. Their dresses show red bars upon white,
black arrow-heads upon green bands, red stripes upon
black or green: they are the most colourful of the race of
women. Also they have bracelets on their arms, and
many rings of silver on their fingers, and each has round
her neck coils and coils of beads—green, blue, red coils
that go from shoulders to chin: twenty pounds weight of

necklace. They bring their hair over their foreheads in mats that are then turned back; their faces are square with copper-coloured soft flesh; their eyes are narrow and unlighted.

The men are resting now and the women are the only folk moving about. What a picture they make as they go quickly and intently across the enclosure or stand before the blazing branches that are their cooking fire! There are three before the blaze now: one holds a hatchet, one a ladle, one a spear-shaped piece of wood: with their purples and puces, their blacks and reds and greens, their square copper faces, they are worth looking at. They move here and there, cleaning fish, cutting up wild duck, attending on pots and kettles. The encampment suggests a gypsy one. But the faces of the old women take on a reddish, not a dark tinge, and the women, young and old, have a detachment from us that is not gypsy-like: they smile and laugh even, but their eyes are as unresponsive as the eyes of otters. They talk in low voices, their words being made up of long collections of syllables.

When I go back of the camp I am in the Everglades. These Everglades are no longer swamps: they have been drained, and the ground with its sparse grass is crinkly where I walk. Trees have been left from the swamp: they are called cypresses, but none could be more unlike the dark voluminous trees that are cypresses for us. They are blanched and abbreviated, and draperies of grey Spanish moss stream from branch and stem. I walk without hearing the sound of a breeze or the stir of

The Country of the Cranes

leaves. The soundlessness of the swamp is in this fantastic forest. And so I come upon another of the canals that drain the Everglades.

And here I see the cranes, or, if you will, the herons. Silver-grey and slate-grey, metallic-blue, white, or with iron-tinged plumage, they stand, or rise, or hover, or droop over the water and its margins. Or they fly through one another's ranks, white and dark wings mingling—a flight to be remembered. Or one by one they drop down on the blanched and abbreviated trees, each taking a tree for its perch. . . . And now I come to where there are tufts of high grass, and here I see the neighbours of the cranes. They are graceful, slender birds with blue-gleaming plumage: they do as the cranes do—fly and settle, each taking a single tree for its perch—blue-gleaming birds on blanched trees. Or they fill up the grass-tufts making a continuous murmur by way of singing. These are the grackles. And now a buzzard heaves himself up from the ground: he had been sitting with red head sunk between his wings. But what a magnificent flyer he is when he gets going! Several, with stretched wings that are tufted with lighter feathers, are now circling over the water the cranes are treading, the flyers searching for dead fish. One settles on a tree, making it seem more blanched and abbreviated. The cranes are taking to the trees too, the egrets trying to distinguish themselves from the others by hovering above a tree with yellow legs drooping. A tall white crane edges to a further distance. A metallic-blue one is treading the water cautiously. Once again

they make flight, and white and dark wings mingle—
such wide, gliding wings—in momentary tumult, and
their cries are as raucous as the caws of rooks. Again
a subsidence, and I watch the quiet watchers standing
here and there, while the egrets stay on the trees.

HENRY FORD VERSUS TOILERS
OF THE SEA

AMONGST the pleasures of staying at the seaside I put first the pleasure of looking at boats in harbour. Each is isolated from our world of striving and enduring; we see it as a magical abiding-place enveloped in a subtler element than the one we tread upon. It moves (I speak now of the boat with sails) with the ease and deliberation that is the very movement of freedom. Many boats with sails are in this particular harbour, white sails and deep brown sails with an occasional lemon-coloured sail, and now and again a patched sail—white patched with brown, or brown patched with white. Sails, I begin to see, are an architecture that completes a boat; sails are a grace in the double sense of being an adornment and of suggesting a spiritual influx. Consider a boat without sails—how primitive, how barely utilitarian; a box or a hollow log. But by putting a sail on it, man allies himself with the most intangible of the elements—air; he uses the air to complete the conquest of the water. And how well the addition becomes his handiwork—a grace indeed! The sail is the happiest of man's inventions; it is the equivalent of the step from prose to poetry, and is actually the step from water into the air. And when a ship with sails moves we must think of it as Ponce de Leon's barque.

Walking down the street that goes by the harbour, I reflect on a statement made by the most influential personage of to-day—a statement that seems to give his general idea of the sort of world he would have. "It matters not what books may be written, what buildings put up, what works of art created—nothing matters if the opportunity be not given for anyone who wills to live as befits a human being." The Henry Ford who expresses himself thus in "To-day and To-morrow" seems to overlook the inner life of man, to take no account of the life of intuition, thought, and meditation, of the life that expresses itself in art and philosophy, and that has been fostered by the great civilizations he discounts so readily. He notes that there is need for a balance in life. But the balance he would have to the life of production has no poems in it, no pictures, no music, no philosophy, no history read through philosophy—there is only the entertainment of knowing trees and birds, of motoring, and of walking across the countryside.

And he has no interest in the other arts—the arts of making serviceable things by the hands in accordance with traditional patterns. I walk down the street of this fishing-village and I look on men mending nets—widespread ones on the beach and smaller ones at the doors of their houses. I look at them building and repairing boats. Women are washing their household laundry in a cistern on the beach into which a stream runs; they spread the things out to dry on another part of the beach; then they wheel them home in barrows. Other women are knitting outside the doors of their houses. Each house shows an interior that is a work-room; always one sees heads bent over a piece of work, the worker sitting beside a fine press or dresser with a shrine above. These presses and dressers and beds look as if they had been built to resist the elements. The openings that ornament the panels of the presses are cir-cular and with spokes—the steering-wheel of a ship. The plates on the dresser are brilliant in lustre and have a design that recalls the wickerwork of the fishing-baskets. Here are arts which this great prophet of in-ventiveness takes no stock in, arts for which there is indeed no room in his world.

No political leader has made such a change in peo-ple's lives or has created such a world of new interests as has the man whose book I have read in these sur-roundings. And no writer, thinker, or philosophical scientist has affected the habit of thinking of millions of people as he has done. He is meeting, it would seem, not only a world's want but a world's longing; it is as though men and women were finding some hope of theirs realized in the machinery he is giving them—machinery that can be handled by the least expert amongst them. And this production of machinery is only one side of the revolution he is bringing about. The other side is through his conception of business. "Low wages will break business far more quickly than they will labour," he writes. And again, "The right price is not what the traffic will bear. The right wage is not the lowest sum a man will work for. The right price is the lowest price an article can steadily be sold for. The right wage is the highest wage the employer can steadily pay." Once more, "Industry is not money—it is made up of ideas, labour, and management, and the natural expression of these is not dividends, but utility, quality, and availability. Money is not the source of any of these qualities, though these qualities are the most frequent source of money." And then, "It matters not what books may be written, what buildings put up, what works of art created—nothing matters if the opportunity be not given for anyone who wills to live as befits a human being."

But surely it does matter. There never was a time in human history when every man, woman, and child in any society had what Henry Ford would regard as decent food, shelter, and clothing. There never was an epoch in which opportunity was given to anyone who willed to live in a way that Henry Ford would regard as befitting a human being. And yet we know that there were and are civilizations. Civilizations are nothing else than the effort made by human societies to reclaim men from the wildness of nature, to focus their minds upon certain ideas that are beyond the providing of food, clothing, and shelter—metaphysical ideas—and by attaching them to these ideas to enhance whatever they possess of an inner life. None of them have given an opportunity to everyone who willed it to live as befits a human being. But the very conception of what befits a human being is due to civilizations, is due to what has been achieved through books, buildings, and works of art.

We must have the efficient factory and the machine. But we must relate them, as the productions of other civilizations were related, to some metaphysical, to some religious idea. Otherwise those who belong to them, those who produce them will have their lives externalized, their inner lives diminished, will have, perhaps, satisfactions, but not that delight in life that one can detect even in the complaining farmer in a European countryside. Externalization of the worker's life may increase productiveness, may make comfort of a kind more widespread, but it may also lead to unhappiness as great as any that has come upon society. . . . Here I watch men making their nets and their baskets, their boats and their barrows; I watch women making their household's stockings, and I have the feeling that the men and women engaged in these tasks are enriching some part of their being. These works, done in the open air, in sight of the village that they and their fathers have lived in and will go on living in, knit generations together and help to form fellowships; they are works of piety in the old sense of the word, for their makers put their personalities into what is meant to be helpful, and the works themselves produce in us a reverence for what has been done by men's hands. Henry Ford would abolish these household arts; he would have baskets, barrows and boats, nets and stockings, made in great factories where the workers, according to carefully planned schedules, produce things which are for

A Half-Day's Ride or Estates in Corsica

everybody and so for nobody, things which neither their children nor their neighbours use. I think that in abolishing these household arts he would abolish not only work that busies people in a natural and pleasing way and helps to keep local economists free from the spectre of adverse trade balances, but a part of human virtue. As I watch men knitting a wide-spread net where the murmur of the sea makes an accompaniment to their talk I sympathize with the extravagance of tone that is in one of Rainer Maria Rilke's poems, in the poem in which he declares that the only memories of earth that we may bring to the angels should be of what we have seen done by men's hands—

Sing of the earth to the angel; not ineffable earth,
To him can you boast of no rapture.
You are but lately arrived
  in a world where he feels so much more.
Show him rather the simple man-made things
  that race after race have fashioned, and that live
  still, in our sight and near to our hands.
Tell him of things. He will stand beside you and wonder
  as you once stood in Rome by the maker of rope,
  or by the potter in Egypt.
Show him how happy a thing can be, how blameless, how much
    ours.[1]

Still I mustn't imply that these villagers are unsympathetic to or uninfluenced by the mechanists and the mass-producers. Their houses have electric lights. They have power-boats. They have automobiles. And, alas,

[1]"Elegies of Duino": translated by Hester Pickman.

they have gramophones. All these, however, are on the outside and could be taken away from them without leaving much sense of loss. These mass-produced things have not altered their outlook nor their feeling about the world and about life. The figure of the Crucified looks over the harbour and the prayer is at the foot of the Cross: "Guide our mariners; protect our fishermen!" The "tragic sense of life" which Henry Ford's philosophy does not include is felt here. And because there is such a sense the people can live with conviction and face death without evasion—that is, with dignity. Against that background they can have hope, contentment, happiness, and not merely a succession of "good times."

And now there are steps upon the street that sound like those of the Gods of the Mountain in Lord Dunsany's play. They are the steps of men coming back from the fishing; they pound along, two by two, carrying between them baskets filled with their catch. And, as is proper in a scene that has ships for its background, many wooden-legged men are around.

Well, blue-bloused pair after blue-bloused pair, the fishermen are here with last night's catch. The women gather around it, black aprons over black dresses, black shawls enveloping their heads, their faces very lined and very alive; they keep up a debate that sounds like the never ceasing crying of gulls. They make a very stirring sight, these women in the sheds with fish piled or in baskets before them. One woman is gutting a dog-fish—a long, spotted, snake-headed spoiler that has broken many nets and devoured whole shoals of fish. Piled in baskets are mackerel of all sizes, elegant in shape and looking handsomer now than they will look an hour hence; their bellies are pure silver, their backs a patterned blue, and their scales have the iridescence of the armour of an enchanted knight. The soles have shapes that one could easily cut out of paper. In the long baskets are oysters so brown and earthy-looking that it is hard to believe that the sea ever flowed over them. Scattered on a bench, their red specks showing, are the mullet. And in the harbour boats with sails move with the ease and deliberation that is the very movement of freedom.

PLAUTUS AND THE COMIC INHERITANCE

Flour on his face, with a derby hat on, a black jacket and flowered pantaloons over his tights, the patron presented himself as the clown. He and his wife (she had made no change in her house-dress) clowned it sufficiently to get the children pleased; then he made his announcement. It was to the effect that a seat on the benches was thirty sous, and that upon a sufficient number of them being occupied the show would begin. He was an Italian, the type that has appeared in every version of the Strolling Players, with a voice that suggested that he might have been a singer; a competent actor, too, in usual rôles. These pitch-people had come in wagons that were houses on wheels—bright yellow bodies with red wheels. The bigger wagon was automotive and dragged the other on. It was lighted when I first noticed it; within was a supper-table with bottles of wine. A horseshoe of benches had been formed: poles had been set up. When I came to the place again the personnel were beating on a drum, blowing into a bugle, clashing cymbals together. They were three: a middle-aged man who was the patron, a woman who was evidently his wife, and a young man. The poles held trapezes; there was a platform under them and a carpet spread for acrobatic feats. The audience had appeared; they were mainly crowded back of the benches,

[107]

but a few were seated—infants, little boys and girls, a mass of grown people.

It must be an anxious life, that of these three strolling players: rain can put them out of business any evening; the patron was well into middle-age and must be getting less and less agile on the swings; a chilly evening could bring on rheumatism. The woman takes care that the men get their overcoats on immediately, and the wagon-house shows considerable comfort; still, it was not surprising that the patron put a good deal of urgency into his announcement. There was no rush to the benches, however. Behind them the main part of the audience wondered why they should pay thirty sous when their neighbours didn't. The patron reduced the demand to twenty sous—twenty sous wasn't much, but he'd let them off with twenty sous for the sake of having the benches filled up. He took a plate and went round collecting.

He set down the plate before his wife who made shrugs of disgust. She was a Frenchwoman and knew how to harangue the crowd before her. She told them what she thought of their mean-spiritedness—trying to see a show such as theirs without paying money. Very truculently she went among them with the plate; she drew in some more sous. There was a scene over the plate when she went back; she was scornfully vociferous while her companion made drama of being indulgent in the Italian style. Meanwhile the younger man got ready for his performance. On his behalf the patron addressed the audience, bidding them remember that

the sight of empty benches is disheartening to performers, and that those who have to engage in dangerous feats
have to be put in heart—have to have "spirito" given
them.

The young man did his acrobatic feats on the platform
to an audience hushed on the part of the elders, rapt on
the part of the children. Carried away by his somer-
saults and contortions, more and more of the audience
slipped on to the benches. The patron then gave his exhibition. It was on a high swing; it was done to a pat-
ter that went very well with the audience. "Oh, what
we have to do to earn a living!" "If my poor mother
could see me now!"—this as he balanced himself on a
ladder across the swing. Immediately off the trapeze,
with overcoat on, he picked up a little saucepan and
made his way through the crowd outside the benches.
"Open your purses for a poor man with a family of
twenty-four children and a dog that won't leave him.
Something to get soup. Something to get macaroni."
The hard-fastened French purses were opened this time.
He must have got enough to have raised "spirito" in
him, for when he appeared as the clown once more, his
face white as an egg, a red something that was between
a night-cap and a fez on his head, and a long black
coat on, he was able to do his stuff with zest. But now
the surroundings and not the piece he performed held my
attention.

A lamp burning in the open air showed the white-
faced mime and lighted up a setting that was in itself
spectacular: there was the horseshoe of people, all held

by an expectancy that came through the worn utterance,
the worn gestures, the worn intonations of the player—
old women with high black head-dresses or little white
lace caps, their faces filled with lines, their headgears
alternating black and white; blue-clad fishermen; girls
with knitted shawls of white and blue; children in all
colours, the infants being held up on men's shoulders,
and all with the night and the sea around them. A very
little way beyond the crowd was the Calvary, and alongside were ships that were soon to sail with fishers to New-
foundland or Greenland, their tall masts crossed by
folded brown sails. On the other side, open windows
high up in houses held people—these were like painted
groups of spectators. I remembered this setting when
I had forgotten what the piece was about.

Afterwards when I read Plautus in translation I reminded myself of the scene. These comedies were not
produced indoors for a more or less decorous audience;
they were produced in the market-place, with people
standing in the sunlight to watch them, or seated on
a horseshoe of benches, or looking out of windows, or
mounted on public monuments. For that reason one
should be inclined to ask of a play of Plautus's, "Is
it good circus?" rather than "Is it good theatre?" Un-
less we remember the ring-master and the clown we shall
get no flavor from these whipped-up speeches. And un-
less we have a memory of the circus, Pyrgopolinices,
Miles Gloriosus, and his parasite Artotrogus will be too
tiresomely absurd—

Plautus and the Comic Inheritance

And that elephant from India, for instance! My word, sir!
how your fist did smash his forearm to flinders!
Eh? Forearm?
His foreleg, I should say, sir.
'Twas but a careless tap.

. . . . . .

And how about that time in Cappadocia, sir, when you would
have slain five hundred men all at one stroke? if your sword
had not been dull?

Ah, well, they were but beggarly infantry fellows, so I
let them live.

An intellectual idea has been put into The Haunted
House, whether by Plautus or by the Athenian comic
dramatist from whom he adapted it, and by virtue of
that idea the play is more of the theatre and less of the
circus. An attempt is made to identify human life with
a house. The idea is expressed by the young Athenian
gentleman who is the central character—

Now I want to go on and state why you should think men are
similar to houses. Now in the first place, parents are builders
of their children. They lay the foundations of their children's
lives. They rear them, do their best to instruct them solidly,
and spare nothing necessary to making them useful and orna-
mental as men and citizens. Money spent on this they don't
count expense. They put on the finishing touches—teach them
literature, the principles of justice, law, expend their money
and their labour striving that others may pray for their own sons
to be like them. . . . Myself now—while I was in the builders'
hands, I was always a steady, serious-minded chap. But after I

moved into my own disposition, I ruined the builders' work instantly and entirely. A spirit of idleness came over me. That was my storm. Coming upon me heavy with hail, it instantly beat down and bared me of my poor coating of modesty and morals.[1]

It seems that as it is delivered this long speech is clowned—Philolaches is maudlin as he makes it, and he probably staggers as he speaks. He has, as is usual, spent his substance upon a favourite courtesan. And as usual there is the wily slave to find a way of fooling the father and fixing things so that the lovers are united. The house is haunted, the home-coming father is told it is dangerous for him to go into it, or even to put his hand on the door. It is a good situation for slap-stick comedy. But besides the slap-stick stuff there is the scene between the courtesan and her attendant which has something in it which brings it close to the comedy of manners.

There is a line in Plautus's successor, Terence, which, seeing it as a quotation, I have thought to be as significant as anything in Molière—"I am a man; nothing human is alien to me." How did a line that suggests such a range of feeling and idea get uttered in the modified circus that was the Latin comedy? I have found that the answer is that it didn't get uttered in the sense that we have read into it. By making an isolated quotation of it we have changed the meaning of the line, as I discover when I look it up. "Why do you wear yourself out labouring like this?" a neighbour says to a re-

[1] English translation by Paul Nixon: Loeb Library.

morseful father. "What business is that of yours?"
the Self-tormentor returns. "I am a man; nothing human is alien to me." Said in this context the line has
nothing of the profundity we read into it: no unprecedented person is projected: the Self-tormentor's neighbour has said something that is bound to meet with approbation from an audience, but he is not designed to
be more than a typical neighbour.

In Paris I went to see "La Mauvaise Conduite," a
modernization of a Plautus play produced by the Vieux
Colombier Theatre. The principal male characters wore
masks while the courtesan and her attendants were
dressed like bathing beauties who have been brought
on the scene before they got the whole of their costumes
on. The masks that the men wore identified them with
characters in the current comic strips; their clothes were
modern but stylized. The lines were delivered as if the
characters were in the circus-ring, and the sense of something performed in the open air was suggested not only
by the water-front represented but by the conduct of
the people on the scene; they had the rowdiness of
gamins. Characters belonging to the Commedia dell'
arte were added to Plautus's characters—notably the
Doctor who is overburthened with his learning.

Plautus kept close to the circus, but the characters
that our comedy thrives on are already in his plays—
the Braggart Warrior who becomes the Captain in the
Commedia dell' arte, the father who becomes Pantaloon,
the slave who becomes the valet, the attendant who

becomes the confidant, the young lover who becomes Pierrot—the Scaramouches and the Scapins are to be found in his comedies. Plautus, I suppose, took over from the Greek his stock of types. He handed them on to the Italians, and the Italians presented Europe with them. Then Molière took hold of three or four of them and let us look at the world through their eyes; he took them out of the circus and placed them definitely in the theatre.

His people are types, of course. But that is only to say that he knew what the writer of the "literary" play does not know—that is that it is the business of the writer for the theatre to take a type and enrich it. Characters in plays should be, as actors always are, animated masks. The audience must be able at once to identify the person on the stage—"Who is he? Who is she? Prince, Dreamer, Virgin, Courtesan?" If the dramatist is "literary"—that is, if he is not really of the theatre, he will not discover the mask that permits us to identify and so go with his personae.

ROBERT BURNS AND THE POETIC
INHERITANCE

ROBERT BURNS was the last poet of our tradition to make poetry out of his own works and days. He finds a poem when his ploughshare turns up a daisy's root or a mouse's nest, when Mailie, his sheep, comes to meet him, when he sits down to blackguard his neighbour, when he goes to a penny dance and bestows his attentions on Eliza or Jean or Nancy. "Leeze me on rhyme!" The wonder is that so little of what he made with such abandonment is indifferent poetry. The volume of his work is a testimony to his wide responsiveness and his splendid power of shaping all he felt; it is an index, too, to the culture of the little community that had him for its laureate.

Walt Whitman would have liked to write as Burns wrote—about the days and works of a man who made a living with his hands. But Whitman had a thesis, and this, although it was a thesis about average life, made him a separate man. Burns had no principle that separated him from anyone in his community except the men with theses—the elders and the Calvinistic divines. Besides, Whitman in America could not be a communist in poetry; he might bestow but he could not share, for there was no popular poetry to take from.

A Half-Day's Ride or Estates in Corsica

Burns's mind moved among communal creations; around him were the folk-melodies that, as one might almost say, are the only begetters of lyric poetry; the popular verse-forms that anonymous poets had evolved; the fragments of folk-song that might give rise to new creations or be used to fill out a half-personal combination, half-formed characters, and half-shaped stories.

Like all who have few possessions, Burns's people were interested in things more than in ideas, and like all country people they took account of personalities and phrases. Such tendencies make a good environment for a poet. Their culture was not predominantly Anglo-Saxon; Burns, like the Irish poets of the nineteenth century felt the flow of Gaelic tradition. The music on which he moulded his verse was Gaelic music, and the language he used was influenced by Gaelic memory. This influence is very apparent in the diminutives that are so abundant in his idiom: with these diminutives he creates a language that is often far removed from English speech—

> Wee, sleekit, cow'rin', tim'rous beastie,
> O what a panic's in thy breastie!
> Thou need na start awa' sae hasty,
>   Wi' bickering brattle!
> I wad be laith to rin and chase thee
>   Wi' murd'ring pattle!

His Gaelic affiliations are marked in the measures of his poetry. He writes easily to tunes that come to him from Ireland directly, as in his verse accompaniment to "The Humours of Glinn"—

Robert Burns and the Poetic Inheritance

Their groves o' sweet myrtle let foreign lands reckon,
  Where bright-beaming summers exalt the perfume!
Far dearer to me yon glen o' green breckan,
  Wi' the burn stealing under the lang yellow broom.

And the mould of Irish music is apparent in the vaga-
bond-soldier's song in "The Jolly Beggars"—

I am a son of Mars, who have been in many wars,
  And show my cuts and scars wherever I come:
This here was for a wench, and that other in a trench
  When welcoming the French at the sound of the drum.

He was of Gaelic extraction; Burns was a name assumed
by his family, whose original was a Gaelic one.

Whoever touches Burns's book touches a man and
touches a community and a territory. Here is the heather
expanse where the grouse crops, the meadow through
which the hare limps, the upland which the poet ploughs,
the field in which Mailie, the sheep, met disaster. We see
the creatures of the open with the eyes of the hunter, the
farmer, and the poet, and they are made so familiar to us
that we can well suppose them to sympathize with human affliction—

Mourn, ye wee songsters of the wood,
Ye grouse that crap the heather bud,
Ye curlews calling through a clud;
    Ye whistling plover;
And mourn, ye whirring paitrick brood:
    He's gane for ever!

What uproar arises from the ale-house! What laughter
and vows and recriminations from the place where lov-

ers walk! Carts creak upon the roads; the cattle make
their way back to the byre; the sheep move up the
hills; a drunken piper goes along the road; a fiddler
plays coming from the fair, and a girl sings as she goes
milking. We are made free of a community, and we know
the coarseness and the fervour, the narrowness and the
license, the humour, the natural grace and long-de-
scended refinement that are close to the soil. And then
we sit on a stool in Poosie Nancy's, and rollicking with
the Jolly Beggars know something of the zest of life that
blackguards and starvelings know—the gaiety of the
lost, perhaps, or the liberation that opens us to wisdom.
And at the end we hear the Dead March being played,
and a military volley being fired over the grave of the
poet who recorded it all.

Then let us praise his judgment, his loyalty, his independence—the judgment that made him know the
value of the life he experienced, the loyalty that kept
him close to his own people, the independence that kept
him clear of pseudo-classicism. And let us praise, too,
his lusty devotion to his craft—

> Leeze me on rhyme! It's ay a treasure,
> My chief, amaist my only pleasure
> At hame, a-fiel', at work or leisure,
>   The Muse, puir hizzie,
> Though rough and raploch be her measure,
>   She's seldom lazy.

> Haud to the Muse, my dainty Davie,
> The warl' may play you mony a shavie,

Robert Burns and the Poetic Inheritance

But for the Muse, she'll never leave ye,
    Though e'er so puir,
Na, even though limpin' wi' the spavie
    From door to door!

Turning from Burns's volume I come on a collection
of folk-songs from America—"English Folk-songs of
the Southern Appalachians" which have been collected
by Olive Dame Campbell and Cecil Sharp, and I find
indications in it of the sort of life out of which a Burns
might have come. The Southern Appalachians include
parts of the states of North and South Carolina, Tennes-
see, Virginia, West Virginia, Kentucky, Alabama, and
Georgia: the people seem to be homogeneous and to
have a character and culture of their own. Their number, excluding city-dwellers, amounts to three million
people. In present-day Europe they would form a national group with a representative at the League of
Nations.

These mountain people are regarded as direct descend-
ants of the original settlers who migrated from North
England between one and two centuries ago, and have
been cut off from the outside world since: they are still
speaking the language and singing the traditional songs
of eighteenth century England. Theirs is a closed life
poetically. The original stock they brought over (it
must have included a few Irish songs: the use of the
word "colleen" in "Lady Isabel and the Elf Knight"
and the presence of a well-known Irish ballad, "Willie
Reilly," suggest this) has not been overlaid by any
novel creations. Realism—that is the approach to the

[119]

A Half-Day's Ride or Estates in Corsica

rendering of the familiar environment of the American mountaineers—has come through variants of these old English and Scottish songs. "What have you eaten, Lord Randal, my son?" the mother asks in our best-known version of the ballad. "Eels and eel-broth. . . . Mother, make my bed soon, for I'm sick at the heart, and I fain would lie down." "It's what did you eat for breakfast, Jimmy Randal, my son? . . . It's cold pie and cold coffee. Mother, make my bed soon, for I'm sick at the heart and I want to lie down."

Variants now and again must have satisfied the craving for personal expression—

> When your heart was mine, true love,
>   And your head lay on my breast,
> You could make me believe by the falling of your arm
>   That the sun rose up in the West.
>
> There's many a girl that can go all round about
>   And hear the small birds sing,
> And many a girl that stays at home alone,
>   And rocks the cradle and spins.
>
> There's many a star shall jangle in the West,
>   There's many a leaf below,
> There's many a damn that will light upon the man
>   For treating a poor girl so.

Here the theme is known and the mould is made, and it is by the varying of a simile that these verses have come into being. A garden gone back to the wild—that is the impression that the poetry of "English Folk-songs from the Southern Appalachians" makes upon a reader. The stock is running into lowly forms—

> O turn your back to the billowy waves,
> Your face to the leaves of the tree,
> For it ill becomes an outlandish knight
> Should view a stark lady.

This may be a too-familiar flower, but it is a flower.

How is it, then, that given this homogeneous culture, this tradition of music and song, this people have produced no poet to record their lives in terms of their traditional art—no cousin of Robert Burns?[1] It is, I suppose, because there is no differentiation in their culture, no contrasting (yet not alien) element that could prove fertilizing, no culture in the sense of a metropolitan outlook that has been formed by an awareness of philosophy, art, and high politics inside and outside their own boundary, with a national consciousness added. Such a culture is necessary if there is to be a crystallization, if a traditional poetry, originally the creation of individual poets and now become communal, is to be precipitated into new forms which will express again individual feelings. Robert Burns in Edinburgh, in society, was a stranger. But without the existence of that capital, the existence of that society, he would not have written the poetry that we remember.

Cecil Sharp, in the introduction to the Appalachian

---

[1] There is a poem dealing with the lives of the Appalachian folk that is memorable and distinctive, but it is by a poet who has come to them from the outside—the poet is Percy MacKaye, and the poem is "The Gobbler of God."

songs, marks an interesting contrast between such traditional songs as he has gathered and the cowboy ballads
which have also been collected. "The cowboy has been
despoiled of his inheritance of traditional song; he has
nothing behind him. When, therefore, he feels the need
of self-expression, having no inherited fund of poetic
literature upon which to draw, no imaginative world into
which to escape, he has only himself and his daily occu-
pation to sing about, and that in a self-centred, self-
conscious way, e.g., 'The cowboy's life is a dreadful life,'
'I'm a poor lonesome cowboy,' 'I'm a lonely bull-
whacker,' and so forth. Now this, of course, is precisely
what the folk-singer never does. When he sings his aim
is to forget himself and everything that reminds him of
his everyday life; and so it is that he has come to create
an imaginary world of his own and to people it with
characters quite as wonderful, in their way, as the elfish
creations of Spenser." This collector of folk-songs believes in the nationalism of art. Culture comes from
inheritance and not from education, he maintains. This
is an idea which educationalists in America are trained
to disregard. In the larger cities, at any rate, teachers
are too ready to ignore the educational and cultural
value of the national heritage which practically every
emigrant brings with him to his new home, and to rest
too confidently upon their educational system, which is
often almost wholly utilitarian and vocational. I think
it proper to write down Cecil Sharp's words. "I admit
that the problem which faces the educationalist in America is a peculiarly difficult one, but it will, I am con-

vinced, never be satisfactorily solved until the education given to every foreign colonist is directly based upon, and closely related to, his or her national inheritance of culture."

IT'S NOT ALWAYS EASY TO MAKE
UP A STORY

So SAID the Merchant's Son who was the owner of the Flying Trunk. He was under considerable difficulties, to be sure, for the story he was called upon to make up had to be instructive enough to please the Queen and jocose enough to make the King laugh. Still, even apart from these special difficulties, it is not always easy to make up a story. To arrange certain properties in such a way as to give the illusion that an imagination is at work and a real story is being told—it is easy enough to do this, and the author of "The Flying Trunk" left a lot of such usable properties lying about—flowers that talk and knowledgeable birds, little mermaids and mother's tears that could melt the icy heart of Death—and they have been used lavishly by writers of our day together with openings such as "In China, as you know, the Emperor is a Chinaman, and all the people round him are Chinamen too." Yes, so easily, and therefore so often, have stories been made up by the use of such properties that when we go back to Hans Christian Andersen we are often out of patience with some types of stories that he was the originator of. But we have only to go a little way to come upon some sentence that is so far beyond the reach of the property-manipulator that our delight

[124]

It's Not Always Easy to Make Up a Story,

in this original is restored, as when, in "The Little Mermaid," the bubbling of the Witch's pot becomes "like the sound of crocodiles weeping." Then even through the translation we divine an inimitable way of writing, and we remember that a Danish critic spoke of Andersen's "graphic, crooning, living, dancing, jumping style." It is not always easy to make up a story, and he who would make up one that will be remembered for generations has to do more than arrange properties and play up the arch and the whimsical; he has to create a living, a personal way of writing. When we read, even in a translation in which little care has been taken to bring out a special rhythm, "The Wind's Story"—the story about Waldemar Daa and his daughters—we know that Hans Christian Andersen has a living and a personal style; we move with the element he writes of, we hear its soughing, we feel the spaces it has gone over. "I came back again; I often came back across the Island of Funen and the shores of the Belt and took up my place on Borreby shore close to the great forest of oaks. The ospreys and the wood-pigeons used to build in it, the blue raven and even the black stork! It was early in the year, some of the nests were full of eggs, while in others the young were just hatched. What a flying and screaming was there! Then came the sound of the axe, blow upon blow; the forest was to be felled."

The world he belonged to is far away from the world of the fanciful writers who make up a story by arranging properties he has left. Just before the middle of the nineteenth century he was in the city of his adoration,

A Half-Day's Ride or Estates in Corsica

Rome. He saw the Pope bless the people who stood before Saint Peter's, and he noted that the blessing was given and received as though the people had been "Protestant strangers." "When I was here thirteen years ago, all knelt." The scene outraged his feelings, but then, with habitual optimism, he added, "but in all that happens, everything is for the best." What he was looking on was a symptom of a change that had come upon the world, a change that would render forever impossible a life such as he had had—a life that was like a fairy tale. Democracy was coming into being, and the aristocratic order was passing. "Rome is not the Rome it was thirteen years ago when I was first here. It is as if everything was modernized—

Grass and bushes are cleared away. Everything is made so neat; the very life of the people seems to have retired. I no longer hear the tambourines in the streets, no longer see the young girls dancing their Saltarello, even in the Campagna intelligence has entered by invisible railroads; the peasant no longer believes as he used to . . . ten years later, when the railways will have brought cities still nearer to each other, Rome will be yet more changed.[1]

The democratic, industrial, rationalist, standardizing order was even then emerging; the aristocratic order with its privileges and its ceremony was being thrust aside. In that order there was much that was intolerable, but there was in it, too, something that led it to foster the exceptional individual. It knelt before its popes, it saluted

[1] Hans Christian Andersen: "The True Story of My Life." Translated by Mary Howitt.

[126]

It's Not Always Easy to Make Up a Story

its kings, it did homage to its privileged personages. But these very exercises prepared it to give genuine reverence to poets, to singers, to painters, to sculptors. How often in Andersen's autobiography do we hear of such homage being paid—

The people drew Thorwaldsen's carriage through the streets to his house, when everybody who had the slightest acquaintance with him, or with the friend of a friend of his, thronged around him. In the evening the artists gave him a serenade, and the blaze of the torches illumined the garden under the large trees, there was an exultation and a joy which was really and truly felt.

Jenny Lind was the first singer to whom the Danish students gave a serenade : torches blazed around the hospitable villa where the serenade was given : she expressed her thanks by again singing some Swedish songs, and then I saw her hasten into the darkest corner and weep for emotion.

I reached Perpignan . . . The human crowd moved in waves beneath my windows, a loud shout resounded ; it pierced through my sick frame. What was that? What did it mean? "Good evening, Mr. Arago!" resounded from the strongest voices, thousands repeated it, and music sounded ; it was the celebrated Arago who was staying in the room next to mine ; the people gave him a serenade. Now this was the third I had witnessed on my journey.

I was invited by the students of Lund to visit their ancient town. Here a public dinner was given me ; speeches were made, toasts were pronounced ; and as I was in the evening in a family circle, I was informed that the students meant to honor me with a serenade.

A Half-Day's Ride or Estates in Corsica

There was an eagerness then in all circles and in all places to receive the work of a man or woman of genius. Our democratic and industrial civilization has made us put away the habit of reverence on which such appreciation was based: when there are demonstrations nowadays for a man or woman who might represent Thorwaldsen or Jenny Lind, they are not so disinterested, nor so spontaneous, so friendly, nor so understanding.

It should have been less difficult then to make up such stories as Andersen told, for the people he came from had in those days a life of their own; they had their stories, songs, and music, their hereditary occupations and costumes. Little towns were not then dependencies, on the metropolis. Andersen was born in the little town of Odense. It is only twenty-two miles from Copenhagen, but Copenhagen in those days seemed to be in another country. There was a little theatre in the town where plays were produced in German; it was possible for a boy to grow up in Odense with a passion for and with some knowledge of the theatre and the sort of poetry that belongs to the theatre, and at the same time to have his connection with a local and popular life that had its own distinctive literature, its own distinctive tradition.

Poverty, by shutting away multiplicity, can endow familiar things with special intimacy. This intimacy with familiar things could be of use to the story-teller, as the Merchant's Son found when he set out to achieve both instruction and jocoseness in a story about pots and pans and a market-basket. Andersen was brought up

It's Not Always Easy to Make Up a Story

in such poverty. His father and mother had just a room;
his father was a shoemaker, and his mother came of a
family that was so poverty-stricken that the little room
and the scanty earnings of the shoemaker represented
affluence to her. "She, as a child, had been driven out
by her parents to beg, and once when she was not able
to do it, she had sat for a whole day under a bridge and
wept." Back of this poverty there was feeble-minded-
ness on the side of Andersen's father. Indeed, if the
eugenists of our day could have had power then, Hans
Andersen would never have been allowed to come into
the world at all. His father, for all that, was a remarkable man. "He very seldom associated with his
equals. He went out to the woods on Sundays, when he
took me with him—

He did not talk much when he was out, but would sit silently,
sunk in deep thought, whilst I ran about and strung strawberries,
or bound garlands. Only twice in the year, and that in the
month of May, when the woods were arrayed in their earliest
green, did my mother go with us, and then she wore a cotton
gown, which she put on only on these occasions, and when she
partook of the Lord's Supper, and which, as long as I can remember, was her holiday gown.

The boy was happy with his father—

I possessed his whole heart; he lived for me. On Sundays
he made me perspective glasses, theatres, and pictures which
could be changed; he read to me from Holberg's plays and the
Arabian tales; it was only in such moments as these that I can
remember to have seen him really cheerful, for he never felt
himself happy in his life as a handicraftsman.

A Half-Day's Ride or Estates in Corsica

As a child Hans Christian's greatest delight was in making clothes for his dolls. He had a girlish voice when he sang. The passion he showed for the theatre had a girlish intensity in it. And yet he was a lad of great spirit. Once, when he and his mother were gleaning in a field, the bailiff came towards them with a great whip in his hand. The others ran away, but little Hans faced him, and said, "How dare you strike me, when God can see it." He made up his mind, as a young lad, to go to Copenhagen all alone, to support himself there, while he tried to enter the theatre. "I will become famous," he told his mother. "People have at first an immense deal of adversity to go through, and then they will be famous." Well, he failed to make his way into the theatre either as a player, a dancer, or a poet. This was the making of the Andersen that we know. He took to writing stories; he made journeys through France, Italy, and Sweden. He had written a good deal before he struck into his true vein. He was thirty when he first began to write his stories for children—

In the volume which I first published, I had, like Musäus, but in my own manner, related old stories, which I had heard as a child. The volume concluded with one which was original, and which seemed to have given the greatest pleasure although it bore a tolerably near affinity to a story of Hoffmann's. In my increasing disposition for children's stories, I therefore followed my own impulse, and invented them myself. In the following year a new volume came out, and soon after that a third, in which the longest story, the Little Mermaid, was my own invention.

It's Not Always Easy to Make Up a Story

He told his stories from the stage, and in this way he entered the theatre in a rôle of his own. The photograph of 1870 shows him as having the long, mobile, actor's face. As one looks at it one understands why the telling of his stories from the stage was such dramatic entertainment.

He who shaped these stories for children first of all, had humour, poetry, knowledge of the world, a clear sense of form. He is a great writer because he has created a world that we can move in and live in, and Tolstoy and Balzac could do no more. " 'But that is superb,' said the Princess, as she went away, 'I have never heard a finer composition. Listen! run in and ask what the instrument costs.' 'He wants a hundred kisses from the Princess,' said the maid of honor who had gone to ask. 'I think he is crazy,' said the Princess, and she went away; but when she had gone a little way she stood still. 'One must encourage art,' she said. 'I am the Emperor's daughter! Tell him he can have ten kisses, like yesterday, and he can take the rest from my maids of honor.' 'Oh, but we hate to,' said the maids of honor. 'That's all nonsense,' said the Princess, 'if I can allow myself to be kissed, you can too!' " In that little talk we have society girls of all seasons. All impostors are in the pair who set up their loom to weave the Emperor's clothes out of nothing. All people who hold offices are in the Cat and the Hen who were the inmates of the house to which the poor Ugly Duckling came. "And they always said 'We and the world' for they thought they were half the world, and by far the better half." We get a

profound sense of evil from the Witch's dwelling as the
Little Mermaid came to it—

> Behind it lay her house in the midst of a weird wood, in which
> all the trees and bushes were polyps—half animals, half plants.
> They looked like hundred-headed snakes growing up out of
> the earth. All the branches were long, slimy arms, with fingers
> like supple worms, and they writhed joint by joint from the root
> to the farthest point; all that they could seize on in the water
> they held fast and never let go . . . She bound her long, flut-
> tering hair around her head, so that the polyps might not seize
> her.

Andersen's stories have in them a heroism that tran-
scends the military virtue—they have the sort of heroism that one finds in the lives of the saints—indeed the
story of the Little Mermaid and the Princess who wove
shirts for her swan-brothers out of churchyard nettles
remind one of stories about the saints. What heroic
virtue was in this man who made out of his memories
stories which have such humour, such poetry, such keen
and kindly observation! In his own life he must have
seemed something of the fool—but a fool that Shake-
speare might quote from—the fool in King Lear.

His life was really like a fairy story, with real kings
and queens coming into it. However, the greater part
of his Autobiography again demonstrates that a writer's
life is not a subject for a writer to engage upon. Even
Balzac could not make his writers—he certainly could
not make his successful writers—interesting. As Andersen relates it his life as a child is like one of his own
stories, full of pathos, full of poetry, full of moral hero-

It's Not Always Easy to Make Up a Story

ism of a kind. Who can forget his father and mother walking in the woods, his mother going out only "when the woods were arrayed in their earliest bloom," and bringing back with her "a great many fresh beech boughs, which were then planted behind the polished stone"? Who can forget the grandmother who used to tell about her own mother's mother—"how she had been a rich, noble lady, in the city of Cassel, and that she had married a 'comedy-player,' as she expressed it, and run away from parents and home, for all of which her posterity had now to do penance"? Or young Andersen's visits to the asylum in which his grandmother was employed, and his going to where the poor old women had their spinning-room—

With these people I found myself possessed of an eloquence which filled them with astonishment. I had accidentally heard about the internal mechanism of the human frame, of course without understanding anything about it; but all these mysteries were very captivating to me; and with chalk, therefore, I drew a quantity of flourishes on the door, which was to represent the intestines; and my description of the heart and lungs made the deepest impression. I passed for a remarkably wise child, that would not live long; and they rewarded my eloquence by telling me tales in return; and thus a world as rich as that of the Thousand and One Nights was revealed to me. The stories told by these old ladies, and the insane figures which I saw round me in the asylum, operated in the meantime so powerfully upon me, that when it grew dark I scarcely dared to go out of the house. I was therefore permitted, generally at sunset, to lay me down in my parents' bed with its long flowered curtains, because the press-bed in which I slept could not conveniently be put down so early in the evening on account of the room it occupied in our small dwelling; and here, in the paternal bed, lay I in a waking dream, as if the actual world did not concern me.

Such experience made it possible for the writer to find occasionally that it was not so hard to make up a story.

ART AND INFANCY

THE gardens were the Luxembourg. Around the bench I was on, with an assurance that contrasted with the tentative openings of a solitary young thrush, juvenile sparrows were making their debut. It faced a triangular patch covered with broad-leafed ivy; the trees—half a dozen chestnuts—made a little grove. And placed in that grove, having a quietude that statuary on the open lawns did not have, was a bust that had a tall shaft for its base. More interesting than the features the sculptor had modelled was the bas-relief on the shaft—in fact the bas-relief without the bust would have made a charming monument. It showed a little girl giving a puppet-show to an audience of four youngsters: she stands manipulating the strings with both hands, and the audience has every tremor of excitement. *La Comédie enfantine* is inscribed under the bas-relief. I could not discover who the strict-looking personage was to whom the monument is dedicated; the name under the bust is obliterated. I should like to know who had this association with comedy and childhood.

Having looked for some time on this bas-relief with the stains of green-mould upon it, I was able to read with sympathy an editorial which is a denunciation of the rationalist, the modernist scheme of education. It is in an editorial in a newspaper I have with me.

A Half-Day's Ride or Estates in Corsica

"To pretend to teach childhood without first peopling the memory," protests Charles Maurras, "without filling it with fables, with hymns, with songs, with proverbs, rhymes, dates, lists of capes and straits, declensions and conjugations—to wish to utilize the superior faculties before the inferior faculties have been, I do not say furnished or adorned, but used, trained, vivified, is to give too much labor to judgment, to reason, to the critical and logical powers by making them lose many precious hours, and to give them too much fatigue before they are able to apply themselves to materials worthy of them." While I was still on the bench before the little grove I come on another reference to infancy. It is in a notice of an exhibition—"*L'art pour l'enfant.*"

I left the place where, looking on the graceful and lively figures of the bas-relief, I was drawn back to the play-hours of children who knew the histories of the Forty Champions of Christendom and who had permanency behind them—permanency of places, of ideas, of relationships—and went to the exhibition. On my way, to gratify the young person who went with me, I made the ascent of the Eiffel Tower. As I looked down from the first stage, the scene below seemed toy-like. It was not that the people, the lawns, the formed gardens were toy-like because they were diminished (miniatures are not toys); it was because they had taken on the roundness and flatness that the toy-maker always gets into his work. It is not distance, I realized, that makes things toy-like. It is the perspective of height. Toys are things to look down on. The toy-maker is one who lives on a tower. And thinking this over I go into the exhibition.

Attached to it is a small museum; it is dedicated to the memory of the Countess de Ségur—a museum of souvenirs of the generation who were the first readers of *Mémoires d'un âne* and *Un bon petit diable*. Before taking stock of *"mobilier, orfèvrerie, jouet, imagerie"* offered to the children of the present day, I am able to note how the children of the Second Empire were provided for.

Here is a recreation-room of theirs. The wall-paper makes it look like a padded room. On the wall hangs a bird-cage, on the shelf are half a dozen books all in identical red covers. There are two dolls very drably dressed. On the table is a little candle. I have a sense of being shut in and of looking out into a rainy garden. Then I turn to look at the rooms that parents of present-day children can have the experts of famous studios furnish for them.

The little candle in the other room was symbolic. For the present-day rooms have abundance of light. And the lighting itself can be treated as a fantasy: look at the lighting in this room: the bulbs hang in the form of a cluster of bananas that is being looked at by a monkey from the back-wall. In these rooms, to be sure, there are furnishings and decorations which are just novelties—effects which custom would take away the freshness and surprise of: we must be on our guard against being enthusiastic about such. That monkey-puzzle with the amusing monkey hanging from it which makes a decoration for the back of the room—in a while it would seem as ordinary as the bird-cage and the drab dolls. Still, discounting effects such as these, effects which are just novelties, we can say that present-day children have worth-while things offered them— light, uncrowded space, simplicity, fantasy, proportion. As we look into these rooms we are no longer reminded of the miserable sign over journeymen-tailors' shops— "Gents' suits cut down for juveniles." These are not grown-ups' rooms cut down: some sympathetic intelligence has been put into making them places for children, with furnishings and decorations that have relation to children's sizes and minds and some consideration for the ease of growing bodies. And yet I feel that these bright rooms lack something: an element of permanency, of tradition.

For it seems to me that any of these admirable fixtures might be changed to-morrow and something different featured. That richness of tradition which reaches us from the bas-relief of the puppet-show can hardly be associated with rooms such as these. That richness went with a permanency of places, ideas, relationships, even of furnishings. In the other room, the room in the museum, the wall-paper that gives it its padded appearance, the chairs, the shelf, were there for ever. The candle, too—one might say it was there for ever. In every history the children heard or read there was a candle. As I think over this the protest of Charles Maurras's comes back to me: he feels, I suppose, that in children there is an automatic, a passive element; it is

this that should be used, trained, vivified. Well, I can't
imagine this element having much attention given to it
in these expertly furnished rooms.

I should prefer to speak of it as the element which
makes children born spectators, born audiences. No explorer or interpreter of the child mind has made enough
of the fact that children can be and love to be spectators
and audience. It is because they have the sense of
audience that comes from being audience that they
make their play drama. "Go to bed now," said a mother
to a child in a house in the Dublin countryside that I
was in. "Ah, I want to be listening to the chat," said
the youngster. No theatre-frequenter, no lecture-goer
ever expressed such longing for the prolongation of his
excitement, his enlightenment, his pure entertainment.
And what was the "chat" about? About the price of
herrings, the characters in a pub, the politics of road-
repairing. In truth, this passive element, the element
which envelops and keeps "fables, hymns, songs, proverbs, rhymes, dates, lists of capes and straits, declensions and conjugations" is an element in children's
minds which should be acknowledged, respected, and
fostered; it is the element which makes it possible for
any of us to have such an incredible accomplishment as
a human language—to have acquired even two or three
languages in less than fifty moons. I have a notion that
what makes children such absorbed spectators and audiences might flourish better by the light of the little
candle than under the charming arrangement that holds
the electric bulbs in the present-day room.

A Half-Day's Ride or Estates in Corsica

If this be so, we cannot estimate the loss in entertainment and enlightenment to childhood that the departure from the old-time crowded family life with its comings and goings has brought about. Here sits a child watching a woman knitting. The flame on the hearth rises and sinks down; there are shadows on the walls; the clock ticks loudly; the cat drags her kittens about. A man comes in with a load of wood, and a friendly or quarrelsome discussion begins between him and the knitter. These are types that the child will remember, that he will discover in every literature. As he listens to them he learns about human history and human relationships. Rhymes, fables, lists of straits and capes, conjugations and declensions, become part of what he guesses at. He knows about the world as man first knew about it—as myth.

But enough of reverie: let us see what is to be seen in the exhibition and the museum attached to it. We see in the museum magic-lanterns and music-boxes, a view of the London exhibition of 1852, and a miniature drawing-room and kitchen. We realize that the children of past days had possessions as well as playthings—these were not things to get tired of and be discarded. Everything that should be in a drawing-room is in the replica we look into: a lady seated in the centre, a maid standing to make some announcement, a piano with even a sheet of music on it, pictures on the walls, flowers in their vases. The kitchen is even more complete. The cook stands by the stove, and above her head are burnished pans and saucepans, each in proper scale. On the

Art and Infancy

shelves are jars and containers of every kind—a hundred of them, and every one perfectly made. Under the shelves are coops with poultry in them. Everything is there in numbers, and everything is in its place. The child who owned this could have the most delightful time making an inventory of his or her possessions— things and things and things—a whole treasury of familiar things.

The toys made for children of our day have color and fantasy: giraffes and monkeys and teddy-bears and villagers of savage lands. These single toys do not entertain me as much as do the toys made in the École Municipale Boulle—a country railway-station, a market-place, a shepherd's place in the Alps. These toy-concourses are full of liveliness and humour—the porters on the railway-platform wheeling barrows, the friends embracing, the conductor waving his flag, or, in the market-place, the public monument, the traffic policeman, the motor halted, the old women, the geese. A real toy-maker's imagination has gone into these crowded scenes, and they represent new ideas in the craft. I note what types of humanity lend themselves to the toy-maker's art. Soldiers always did. Policemen do. So do railway-porters and train-conductors, and anyone whose profession is familiar and can be indicated simply: it is as an agent of the community that man is toy-like, and, remembering the scene from the Eiffel Tower, I think he has to be seen from the top of something.

TWO POETS

THROUGH the accident of finding their names together in an anthology, these two men—Wilfrid Scawen
Blunt and Bliss Carman—come before me with contrasting features: one a man of the world, an aristocrat
who had taken part in great affairs, who had known the
cities and the men of his time, and the other born in
a province of a colony, living the last twenty years of
his life in an American village, detached from the affairs of the world. Yet if they had met they would have
liked each other greatly, I feel—both had hearts for
causes that the world does not acclaim.

They were both tall men. In Bliss Carman's case
that exceptional bulk was contained in a thin integu-
ment. He bled easily; he was sensitive in every part of
his great frame. However, the irritability that usually
goes with thin skin was no part of his nature. Bliss Carman was above everything else a sweet-natured man. I
am sure no one ever parted from him without saying
"I hope I shall see dear Bliss Carman again." His life
had a frugal dignity that was in itself a rare and fine
achievement. The tweeds that he wore had given him
long service; they were always carefully pressed and
spotless. That wide-brimmed hat he had worn for
many seasons. Yet there was always something in his

attire that corresponded to the gaiety and color of his mind—a bright necktie, a silver chain, a turquoise ornament that some Indian friend had bestowed upon him.

I remember Wilfrid Scawen Blunt in Arab dress— hanging black robes with some gold embroidery upon them. He was in his seventies when I saw him for the first time, with massive stooped shoulders—a figure that made me think of some of the mighty Semitic kings. His eyes were friendly and he had a quiet and humorous speech. Because he was now a lonely watcher, a solitary aider of those who, in many lands, made resistance to the rule of the soldier, the diplomat, and the banker, there was detachment in the way he spoke of many great issues. There was frankness, too; he had been in the state's service; he belonged to a caste which had taken an empire for its preserve; his detachment had something in it of the coolness of the professional giving observations and estimates.

This was in his house in Chapel Street in London. I saw him later in his house in Sussex, in Newbuildings, after he had left London, never, as he told me, to go back there. The aspect of a deserted house was in the approach to Newbuildings—grasses and flaunting weeds were allowed to grow between the steps of the house, and rabbits in hundreds careered around it. There was a room where a fire blazed on the hearth. The walls of this room showed the bare stone, but on one wall, over the stones, was the brilliant Morris tapestry, "The Annunciation," the design of which is by Burne-Jones. In the dining-room was the table that had been William

Morris's: inserted in the board was a plate inscribed with Wilfrid Scawen Blunt's verse praising Morris's companionship and his table-talk. And at Newbuildings was part of Blunt's famous Arab stud. What beautiful horses were in the stables there! Horses roan and chestnut and cream-coloured, horses with delicately shaped necks and eyes of size and beauty! The Sultan of Turkey used to buy horses out of this stud—horses that were better than any to be found in Arabia. The finest Arab horses were no longer in the desert country, Wilfrid Scawen Blunt told me. "The swiftness of his horse," he said, "was an insurance for the Arab—he could escape death on his horse's back. But the rifle has destroyed the effectiveness of that insurance, and the Arab chiefs are no longer interested in keeping up the strain of swiftness." I had just discovered Lyall's "Poetry of the Pre-Mohammedan Arabs," and was eager to talk to him about that great Arabian poetry. He praised the pre-Mohammedan fragments. "I have always said," he remarked, "that Mohammedanism spoiled the Arabs." Then, after repeating some poetry in Arabic, he said, "Arabic is a language to be shouted across great spaces—a language of the open air and the desert." He had written a play based on one of the Irish heroic stories and it had been produced in Dublin. Yeats had written him that if he had begun to write plays in his thirties he would have had a European reputation as a playwright. I said of this play—"Fand" is its title—that the fact that it was in rhymed verse made it seem non-theatrical to a Dublin audience. He remarked with some humour, "Blank verse is essentially English. I departed from it for the sake of the Celtic theme. Surely rhymed verse comes nearest to Celtic form."

Wilfrid Scawen Blunt lived in retirement from a world he had known very well. Bliss Carman was saved from being a solitary by a fine and devoted friendship that had been granted to him. Every morning I would see Bliss Carman walking from his room in the village inn to his friend's house. I lived in the same village at the time. There he would spend the day, writing, reading, walking and dreaming, returning to the village at night. The only utterance I ever heard him make about public affairs was a vigorous denunciation of prohibition. His last poems reflect the house in which he had peace and content and the garden that the wild creatures were not shut out of. He was born in New Brunswick—New Brunswick which, as his comrade of the old days, Richard Le Gallienne, reminded us, "when it belonged to France, went by the more charming name of Acadie, or Acadia, immortalized by Longfellow, and as near to Arcady in its romantic natural features as its name. It is a region of glittering lakes, rivers, and bays, rocky ravines and great forests, abounding in wild life, a paradise of the adventurous canoeist." This delightful province was always in his mind. But his later poetry belongs to New England, to Connecticut, and particularly to "the little valley of the Silvermine." The mood of this poetry is of the day's close, when birds fly close to the hedges and are suddenly present in gardens,

A Half-Day's Ride or Estates in Corsica

when flowers are no longer flaunting and trees are a dim
stature, when the noise of insects in the garden becomes
distinct and men are seen on their homeward way. The
stir of the world is far from this poetry; it was far from
the first poems he wrote—

For a name unknown,
Whose fame unblown
Sleeps in the hills
For ever and aye;

For her who hears
The stir of the years
Go by in the wind
By night and day;

And heeds no thing
Of the needs of spring,
Of autumn's wonder
Or winter's chill;

For one who sees
The great sun freeze,
As he wanders a-cold
From hill to hill;

And all her heart
Is a woven part
Of the flurry and drift
Of whirling snow;

For the sake of two
Sad eyes and true,
And the old, old love
So long ago.

Two Poets

That is the poem of Bliss Carman's that is given in the anthology. Greatly does it contrast with the poem beside it, the poem by Wilfrid Scawen Blunt, that man who possessed and who desired so many things—

> I long have had a quarrel set with Time
> Because he robbed me. Every day of life
> Was wrested from me after bitter strife;
> I never yet could see the sun go down
> But I was angry in my heart, nor hear
> The leaves fall in the wind without a tear
> Over the dying summer. I have known
> No truce with Time nor Time's accomplice, Death.
> The fair world is the witness of a crime
> Repeated every hour. For life and breath
> Are sweet to all that live; and bitterly
> The voices of these robbers of the heath
> Sound in each ear and chill the passer-by.
> —What have we done to thee, thou monstrous Time?
> What have we done to Death that we must die?

I used to see him in his latter days, propped up in his bed in the mornings, writing in pencil, in the clearest and firmest handwriting, the entries in his diary that chronicle the decline of a civilization——the entries that have gone to make his volumes of memoirs. It was greed, he thought, now more unabashed than ever, that was making the world less free and less lovely than it was fifty years before. Men had less and less passion about liberty. He was glad to hear that there was a revival of the military idea in Irish nationalism; he had been made sorry to hear of Irish people of that time——the Home

Rule era—mouthing loyalty to a polity which denied them the right to govern themselves. "I have remained a Fenian," he said. In Egypt the British had built a dam across the Nile and the Temple of Philae was being destroyed by the gathering of the water. And it was all because Manchester wanted Egypt to grow more and more cotton. "The *Times* will exhort us to 'a happy Philistinism' and will comfort us with the remark that the poor fellaheen will have heavier crops. But it will not tell us that Egypt has begun to import grain for the first time in her history, that fevers have come from the rise of the waters, and that contact with us has brought alcohol into the Moslem villages." Hearing him speak dispraisingly of the sons of Highland lords who enter the Guards and dissipate their resources in London, I said, "You don't like people who are not true to their racial heritage." "I hate 'friendlies,'" he said gruffly. Are they final, the judgments which he has put down in his memoirs—these imperturbable judgments on soldiers and priests, writers, statesmen, and administrators? Perhaps not. But they are the judgments of a man who had been in many courts and assemblies, and who, through his many faculties, had lived amongst many kinds of men—as a man of rank, as a man of letters, as a poet, a traveller, and a diplomat; they are, above all, the judgments of a man who had it in him to judge boldly. When we read that series of memoirs which include "India Under Ripon," "With Cromer in Egypt," "The Land War in Ireland," "My Diaries, 1880 to 1914," we are able to turn from the official cinema of history and look at the improvisations that are made in great houses and council chambers—at least as regards the countries that were in the British polity. Everyone writes memoirs, but only one man of our time has been able to write memoirs that have an heroic vein and an epic scope, that Englishman of aristocratic family and Catholic stock who strove for the liberation of the people of Ireland and the people of Egypt and for the self-determination of the Moslem world which he thought could be achieved through an untrammelled Egypt, Wilfrid Scawen Blunt.

THE–CITY–TO–BE–FORSAKEN

OR

THE COLONIAL EXHIBITION IN PARIS THE EVENING BEFORE ITS CLOSE

THE-CITY-TO-BE-FORSAKEN has half a million folk upon its ways: to-morrow it will have only a handful of hirelings and hucksters; then its demolition will begin; a few days more and its temples and bazaars will be bodily removed, and when we are here again we shall know this site for the forest that it was. Enough trees were left to give a background to the buildings and afford a retreat from the marts—clumps of poplars, lines of chestnuts, groves of acacias.

Now on the last day of the city's existence I look towards a column that is very clear in the light of a winter sky. It has the appearance of something aboriginal. Geometrical designs, figures of men and horses incised on the stone carry the eye up to where great buffalo heads with high horns surmount it. I had thought that these horns were about four feet in height: now that I see men standing between them I know they must be about fifteen feet high—the bent buffalo heads about the same: these great horned heads against the sky seem to typify some outlandish pastoral people; the column is the mark of that island-continent, Madagascar. I am on a street of incongruities—a steep conical roof thatched and brown, a temple with malachite turrets, a fortress in reddish clay, a church surmounted by a cross, and then the straight, clear turrets of Islam. The temple represents the one record that a vanished race has left of itself—it is the translation of Angkor Vat. Terrace above terrace it rises up, an architecture of terraces: one feels the absence of cymbals, bells, banners, and gorgeously arrayed processions passing along the terraces and up and down the straight stairways. Beside the grey of Angkor Vat is the reddishness of Africa —a fortress with bulging turrets surmounted by gourd-like cupolas, a primitive edifice, but one made by men who knew how to use their material. Tunisian and Algerian buildings contrast with the temple of unending figures and ornaments—straight unornamented turrets that have light cupolas, buildings open, cool, and spacious. And then such a building as there was in North Africa before Moor and Arab came into their own. Statues of Roman Emperors stand outside, and within it, for frescoes are great picture-maps—Imperium Romanum, showing the Empire, with fasces and the eagle in gold for insignia, and opposite Alma Mater, picturing the City, with the Wolf and Twins, and the potent letters S. P. Q. R.

From this basilica I see the first of the effects which make the night scene in the-City-to-be-forsaken so romantic. A high fountain. Jets and fumes rise from its dozen branches. Now it is illuminated; I see a golden mist above the Lombardy poplars that stand above the fountain. Golden streams fall from its mount-

ing jets and gush from around its base. The play of
water under the lovely lights is enchanting. And now
the streets of the City are illuminated. These lotos-
blooms suspended from white columns are street-lamps.
Farther down, tall pillars with fumes rising from them
and giving multi-colored lights, make illumination.
The rugs, the brass lamps, the water-jars in the bazaars
recall the story-telling of the Arabian Nights. A perfume-seller is crying his wares: as he shakes the glass
tube he has put in one of the jars the air takes perfume
—jasmine or roses. He is a story-teller as well as a
perfume-seller.

THE PERFUME-SELLER'S STORY-TELLING

I stand within a courtyard of Angkor Vat, marvel-
ling at an architecture that makes processions out of
stone. Before me a flight of steps goes up straight as
a pillar almost, and on terrace above terrace paired
Chinese lions stand with heads straight and tails raised
up. There are chariots and great-breasted, slim-
waisted women, ramping lions, rearing horses, warriors
and dancing-girls. And as I look over this incon-
ceivable detail the perfume-seller who was with me
says—

"Now the girl who was brought to Alexander as a
pledge of alliance was not like the daughters of Persia,
languid and brilliant-eyed, nor like those long-bodied
dancers who are the same in every land. Frankly she
stood and frankly she looked around her as if her spirit

was as one of those birds that are curious and daring but that can only be drawn down by some extraordinary lure. An Indian sage was with her. Now Aristotle, and Mazda the Persian, and this Indian sage sat together and talked of the immortality that each of them would gain, and of what conquest each had made to keep his name in remembrance amongst the generations of men. Mazda said he would be remembered for the chant he had made, the chant in praise of Mithra who stands before the sun: all other worships would pass except the worship of the sun and of pure fire; all other philosophies would fail except the philosophy that led men to live the pure and heroic life that Zarathustra taught in his verses; the worship of fire and the words of Zarathustra would spread throughout the world, and where the worship and the words went there would go, too, his chant to him who lifted up the hearts of the Aryan warriors. Then Aristotle spoke about his book on politics, saying that wherever one designed a government fitted for free men, his thought would be heeded. The Indian sage, was silent, but having drunk the wine that Alexander had sent to Aristotle, he said, 'I, O sages, shall go down to posterity for a single action. Yet my name shall never be told. Nameless, I shall be remembered for my deed. Without a name I shall be forever linked with the name of the Conqueror of the world.' After he had said this Aristotle gave much regard to the Indian sage.

"When he went into the King's pavilion those who were with the King were speaking of his alliance with the Queen of the South. Alexander, who had not turned aside for any of the beauties of the world, was impatient for the marriage that would give him the Daughter of the Queen of the South. Her pearl-embroidered vest was open and Aristotle saw a bosom that lifted with a tide of life. 'She is pure fire even as your master is pure fire,' the Zarathustrian said to him then.

"Why was it, Aristotle pondered, that no living thing had ever been permitted to come near the Daughter of the Queen of the South? And pondering upon this, he thought upon the words that the Indian sage had said, 'Nameless, I shall be remembered for my deed. Without a name I shall be forever linked with the name of the Conqueror of the world.' He said, after he had pondered for a while, 'Before the bridal let the maiden be shown the hardness of the desert and the hunt. Go on a chase to-morrow,' he said to the King, 'and let the maiden sit in a chariot and be with the hunt.'

"Alexander rejoiced that this should be, and Aristotle arranged that the Indian sage should not know about their going. So at dawn they went, and the Daughter of the Queen of the South trembled in her eagerness to be with the King. She went beside Alexander. In the King's chariot were the hunting-lynxes and the falcons. They went into the desert when the sun was rising over the world.

"In the brush the beaters found a gazelle asleep and it was brought living to the Daughter of the Queen of the South. So pleased was she with the gentle creature that she took the gazelle in her arms, and held it and kissed it.

"Then the falcons flew. The King came to where the Daughter of the Queen of the South sat under a great rock. In her arms was the gazelle. She showed it to the King—the gentle creature was dead. 'It hath died of fear,' the attendants said.

"The falcons circled around a grey bird that had flown up from the rocks. The falcons flew above the bird and it dropped down beside the Daughter of the Queen of the South. She took the bird to her bosom. She held it and kissed it and ran with it to the chariot where Alexander was with his hunting-lynxes. But when she showed it to the King the bird was dead. 'It hath died of fear,' the attendants said.

"The falcon lighted on her chariot and there they hooded it. And this wild creature, too, the Daughter of the Queen of the South took into her hands. She fondled it and kissed it, and in a while, lo! the falcon was dead.

"This was shown to him, and the King marvelled. Aristotle spoke and said, 'This maiden hath been reared in a forest with a woman-attendant and with the sage who directed the woman attendant. No living creature was permitted to come near her. And now we see that those who came near her have died. This hath been shown as a warning to thee, O Alexander.' But Alexander said, 'This is madness. Behold her as she stands in the chariot regarding the sun! What beauty and what ardency she has! She could enter into Alexander's world or Aristotle's world. She shall be my bride!'

"Then Aristotle saw that the King might not be spoken to again about the maiden. He listened as they spoke to each other: 'Lord, take my life from me, but take me to thee!' 'Thou art victory and life and death to me!'

"They returned from the hunting. Aristotle found a lovely slave-child and sent her to the Daughter of the Queen of the South with a dish of mountain honey, and this was done without the knowledge of the Indian sage. So lovely was the child that the maiden took her and caressed her. And afterwards she kissed the child.

"The King gave orders that all was to be made ready for the bridal. Waiting women came to the pavilion of the Daughter of the Queen of the South, but they went not within, for they heard sobs that came from the breast of the maiden who was to wed Alexander. Aristotle went to her and found her weeping over the dead slave-child. Then he told her how her kiss would be the death of the king, and how, all unknown to herself, she had been reared upon poisons so that she might prove deadly to the Conqueror of the Indies.

"The King waited for his bride. She came not, and he went to her pavilion and found it forsaken. He caused the trumpets to be blown and all the camp turned out to make search for the Daughter of the Queen of the South. But they found her not, and for three days Alexander sat in the pavilion where she had been, his heart sick

with loss and longing. A boat drifted down the river.
Sentries saw the boat and saw a lonely figure in it. No
more was ever seen or heard of her, the maiden who had
come into Alexander's camp from an unknown country, and whose own name was never known."

A fountain plays in the Tunisian courtyard, and we
look upon carpets that are the most pictured of all
carpets—the carpets of Timgad—that hang upon a
wall. Then the perfume-seller says to me—

"That height on which a figure stands is the wall of
a city. It is the city that Alexander did not conquer.
Far-come wanderers told him of it. After he had heard
of that city, King Alexander felt he had gained little
when he had not taken tribute from it.

"One day with a company of soldiers he went from
his camp towards the mountains that were this side of
the Unconquered City. They crossed the mountains;
halfway down they saw the black walls of the city.
They raised the golden horns and blew upon them; they
cried out the name that had such terror in it—the name
of Alexander.

"It was then that that the figure appeared on the
height. He appeared as a man, but he was really an
angel of God, and the four-coloured garments that he
had upon him had the four colours of the wrath of God.
Alexander cried out that he was the King of the World,
and that he had come to take tribute from the city.

"The angel who had in his garments the four colours
of the wrath of God, caused the gate of the city to be

opened, and Alexander and his company of soldiers entered it. And the one who was an angel, but who had
the appearance of a man, brought him to the treasury
of the city, and showed him the coins, the crowns, the
ingots of gold. And he showed him, too, a strange small
stone, about the bigness of the eye of a man. When the
gold was put into the scale—ingots, crowns, and coins
—this small stone weighed all the gold down.

"Alexander took back with him the small strange
stone. And when he had come back into the camp he
showed it to his sages and generals. All the spoil that the
army had gathered could not, they found, weigh down
that small strange stone.

"Now there was in the camp a famous courtesan, and
she was displeased to see that every wonderful and brilliant thing that the army had gathered as spoil was
weighed down by this small stone. The sages and the
generals and the army forgot it was so, but the courtesan
would not forget it. She would go to the Unconquered
City and make discovery there of what might weigh
down the stone that weighed down all the crowns and
coins and ingots of gold. So in a high purple litter, and
with a guard of soldiers, she went across the mountains
and came before the city.

" 'I have come,' she said to the one upon the wall,
'that you may show me what can weigh down the small
strange stone that you gave Alexander.'

"Then the one who had in his garments the four
colours of the wrath of God, took up a pinch of dust and
put it in the scale against the small strange stone. And

the pinch of dust weighed down the stone that the crowns and coins and ingots of gold might not weigh down.

" 'What is this?' asked the famous courtesan.

" 'What Alexander will become,' the angel answered.

"After that she went from the city and came back to the camp of Alexander. But thereafter she whose mirthfulness had been an enchantment in Persepolis and Babylon had but one thought. Always at midnight she would whisper into the ear of her lover the word about the grain of dust that outweighed that which all the spoil they had gathered might not outweigh. And the general who had been her lover would sit in his tent the next day, not caring which way the army went. It was so with many generals, and even with Alexander himself.

"But the council of the army would not have this go on. A word was given, and then she who had been the most mirthful and most beautiful of the women who had revelled in Persepolis and Babylon, was strangled. The army moved on, leaving her hanging there, the small stone stuck into her mouth."

He sold his jasmine perfume to a black-skinned, bearded man. "He is an Ethiopian," he said, "whose forefather was King Solomon. I know but one word in his language, the word that is the Name of God." "That word I know, too," I said. "So impressive it is that when I heard it I wrote a verse upon it." I repeated—

A Half-Day's Ride or Estates in Corsica

He wrote the letters down from left to right,
Not as in Arabic from right to left,
And then pronounced the syllables they made.
And I heard on the Mountains of the Moon
Eagles a-scream, and knew the word I heard
Was the Ethiopian Name of God.

"Egsiabeher," I said, and he answered "Egsiabeher it is." And then he said—

"The Jewish elders know that the Names of God are twenty-seven. They are written upon a stone that is in the depths of the sea. With the least of these names upon his tongue, man could change the flow of creation and put dismay into the host of the angels. God flung down the stone with the names written upon it that a bound might be set to the waters of the sea. But the names of God, it is supposed, are also written upon the hearts of mankind. The learned who hold this opinion tell this story—

"Once an elder, passing through the Temple, saw an ill-clad man in one of the high seats. And because the man showed poverty the elder commanded him to go hence out of the House of God.

"Then the elder went on his way. But outside his house he met one who was Israfel, and upon Israfel was a garment that was red with the anger of God. 'For what you have done this day in turning the poor out of the House of God, the anger of God has fallen upon your house, and your son will be taken from you. I have come to bear hence the young man's spirit,' said Israfel, the Angel of God. And in the band of Israfel the elder saw the sword of the Angel of Death.

"He wept and said, 'To-day my son takes a bride. Would that you might take my life in place of his.'

"They went within the house and the wedding-feast was being prepared. At all that was shown the elder sighed. He would have rent his garments, but he refrained from doing what was unpropitious at the wedding-feast.

" 'Would that I might go in place of my son,' said the elder again. 'But at least, O Angel, let me be the one who will announce thy dread coming.'

"Then the father went to the bride's chamber to tell his son to come forth and meet Israfel, the Angel of God. But he heard the bride and groom whispering to each other within, and hearing them he turned back to the angel.

" 'The sin was mine, O Angel of God,' said the elder. 'On me be thy stroke.'

"Then the garments of Israfel were seen to be more red with the anger that possessed him. 'Will you then, for the sake of the life of your son, yield your life with all your spirit?' he said to the elder. 'I will,' said the elder. 'Then hold your neck for the stroke of the sword,' said the angel.

"Before the door of the bride's chamber the elder stretched himself. Then, instead of stretching out his neck for the stroke of the sword he hunched his shoulders, and as he did he groaned aloud.

"With garments redder still with the anger that was

within him, the angel stretched his hands above him to open wide the door of the bride's chamber. Even as he did there came along the mother of the youth. The father laid his hands upon her garments and he said, 'Surely you, the mother of our son, will give your life for his.'

"And the mother looked upon the angel whose garments were red with the anger that was within him and she looked upon the sword that the angel held, and she looked upon the hand that was outstretched to open wide the door of the bride's chamber, and she said, 'I will give my life rather than that my son should be taken at this time.'

"Then the angel said, 'Stretch out thy neck for the stroke of my sword.' The mother lay on the ground before the door of the bride's chamber. On the step before the door she laid her head. She did not stretch out her neck, neither did she hunch her shoulders, but she groaned as deeply as the father of the youth had groaned.

" 'Not willingly would thy spirit go,' said the angel, and his garments grew redder yet with the anger that was in him, and his hands pushed wide the door, and he went within, into the chamber of the bride.

"And they sat together, these two, on the step of their bed, whispering one to the other, and in whispers they were saying how one would never part from the other. They saw the angel with his garments burning red and with the sword in his hands, and in dread they looked upon him, seated on the step of their bed.

"The groom rose up and took a step towards the angel and then he drew back. He stood trembling there. But the little bride had taken three steps towards the angel, and she stood bravely under his sword.

" 'On me be thy stroke,' said she, 'if thou wilt permit my beloved to live.'

"The angel whirled the sword around his head. He swung it towards her. As the sword went near her the little bride uttered a name, and at that name the sword swung back in the angel's hand.

"Where had she found the name she had uttered? In her heart, perhaps, as she looked into it under the gleam of the angel's sword. And after she had uttered that name the garment of the angel became like ashes, and he went from the chamber and from the house. And looking upon the groom the little bride said the word 'beloved,' and forgot what other name she had uttered.

"But she had uttered a name that had turned the sword of the angel—she had uttered one of the twenty-seven Names of God."

Angkor Vat, with its terraces, turrets, and stairways, becomes a pale golden colour. We walk down a street that is bordered with African carvings—warriors and sorcerers—all solemn, burthened and unrelievable, and I feel that the forest with its terrors is not far distant.

STRANGE NOSTALGIA

To-day at an exhibition of Byzantine art I looked at
a statuette the memory of which keeps coming back to
me. No bigger than a span, it was a head discovered
somewhere in North Africa. The nose gave the impression of a man who could impose something tremendous
on the earth itself—direct the building of the pyramids
and the great wall of China as a single labor—and the
eyes made me think of one who could see across, not
distances of miles, but of hundreds of miles. The eyes
and nose, as compared with the size of the face, must
have been enormous. And yet the artist who made this
strange image did not give the impression that he was
exaggerating particular features: I had the feeling that
these magnitudes were proper, as they might be in a
survivor of a stock different from ours, a stock that our
tradition keeps a dim memory of—the angelic sojourn-
ers who neglected whatever great service they were engaged in for the sake of dalliance with the daughters of
men. Yes, there was something angelic—angelic in the
sense of belonging to another order—in this countenance
carved in I know not what material. It might also be
a likeness of some survival of Atlantean man.

How strange, I thought when Atlantis came into my
mind, is the nostalgia we have for some high and remote

[164]

ancestral region. We will not have it that we came out of the cave and the forest; we want to believe that we are estrays from some splendid and spacious realm. "We are like the children of unmarried mothers, and the secret of our paternity is in the grave," cries Melville somewhere in "Moby Dick." We feel so about our cultural as well as our spiritual origins; always we are striving to legitimize and ennoble them; therefore we look towards high and remote regions. Every people, apparently, has this nostalgia for the fatherland that was greater and grander than the one their present history knows—"The towery gates of Gorias, of Findrias and Falias, and long-forgotten Murias," as an Irish poet sings, knowing that the less is known about such places the more appealing they are, and that to have the names of them only is best of all. It is not only the poets of the race who feel this strange nostalgia: we have all known men who have high degrees in freemasonry, and have discovered by listening to some discourse of theirs that what really keeps them in the craft is the rituals and the queer histories through which they feel themselves connected with some august country—Chaldea, or Egypt, or, for all I know, Atlantis—and these are business or professional men. Plato, then, dealt with a fundamental theme when he wrote about Atlantis; the history he told, or half told, is his most popular work. I turn to it with interest. And now I have become infected with the nostalgia which I thought so strange, and have resolved to read all I can find that deals with lost fatherlands.

Strange Nostalgia

He left off in the middle of a sentence, but perhaps Plato said all that he had to say about Atlantis. "The divine portion in the Atlanteans began to fade away. It became diluted too often and too much with the mortal admixture; human nature got the upper hand. Then they, being unable to bear their great fortune, became insolent and adopted unseemly ways; to him who had eyes to see they began to appear bare, as having lost their fairest and most precious gifts. To themselves they still appeared glorious and blessed, and that at the very time they were filled with unrighteous power." Of course we should like to have been told how the judgment of the gods was fulfilled, and the ways by which Atlantis came to be overwhelmed. But what has a philosophic historian to do with all that? The cycle of Atlantean civilization was complete; it had grown, as Spengler tells us all civilizations grow, as a flower grows, by some inherent power. And then it had faded. Perhaps no one will ever tell us more than Plato has told us about the decay of a civilization. "The divine portion began to fade away. It became diluted too often and too much with the mortal admixture." And perhaps, philosophically speaking, that is as much as there is to be said about the Atlanteans, as it is as much as is to be said about the Babylonians, the Egyptians, and the Greeks and Romans.

But where did Plato get the piece of history on which he philosophized? Or was it a piece of history? Did he invent Atlantis and its civilization, or did he make use of a tradition that was current in Egypt or some

[166]

other land? And if he did, how had the tradition grown up? Was it a reminiscence of Minoan Crete? Or, as some new authorities guess, of "the Hesperian counterpart of the ancient cultural centres of the Orient" that was Tartessus in Spain? Or had the tradition grown up out of that feeling of catastrophe that comes over us when we look across the Western Ocean at some set of sun?

I have found a book the argument of which is that Plato's account of Atlantis is the working-up of old and authentic tradition, just as Geoffrey of Monmouth's tale of Arthur, or Homer's account of Troy, is the working-up of old and authentic tradition. The book is "The Problem of Atlantis" by Lewis Spence. Arthur existed, Troy existed, in spite of the fact that a great deal that is mythical comes into Geoffrey of Monmouth's account and Homer's account of the scenes and the people. "Broadly speaking," Lewis Spence writes, "it is now generally accepted by critics of insight—the others do not matter much—that when a large body of myth crystallizes round one central figure, race, or locality, it is almost certain to enshrine a certain proportion of historical truth capable of extraction from the mass of fabulous material which surrounds it, and when so refined, is worthy of acceptance by the most meticulous of historical purists." This, I am sure, is sound. But in illustrating the argument by Homer and Geoffrey of Monmouth, Lewis Spence, it seems to me, leaves out of account something that is very important. That something is the time-element. Only a few centuries separated the period of Troy from the period of Homer, the period of Arthur from the period of Geoffrey of Monmouth. But between the time of the overwhelming of Atlantis and Plato's time was a period vast enough to baffle all historical record, all historical memory. Atlantis was founded B.C. 7000, he affirms. Let us say that it endured a thousand years, and was overwhelmed with the islands of which it was the capital B.C. 6000. From that until Plato's time there was a period as long as from the First Egyptian Dynasty until to-day. Can we believe that the Atlantean tradition could have persisted through such a vast period of time? It might persist as a story of general disaster, likely enough, but it could not persist as a record holding the actual physical features of the lost land.

Lewis Spence would reply that the tradition embodying the physical features of the Atlantean country did not depend upon the folk-memory for its perpetuation; it was written down, and Plato's account was drawn from documentary evidence. His whole mass of speculation then really rests upon this hypothetical evidence. And it seems to me that not only the author of "The Problem of Atlantis" but all those who make claim for the authenticity of the tradition that Plato embodied, will have to discover and bring to light this very evidence. Where are the documents from which Plato drew his account? They were Egyptian, and apparently it was next to impossible to destroy Egyptian documents. And how is it we have never heard about the tradition except through Plato? There must have been a great deal of interest in the legend in the Greece of Plato's time and in the Roman world afterwards. The Egyptian priests would surely find it profitable to gratify the curiosity of people interested, even if they were only interested in finding out how Plato's story ended. And yet Plato's is the only account of Atlantis that we have. Herodotus has nothing to say about it. Herodotus had a nose for just such a story, and when he didn't tell it to us we may take it that there was no story about Atlantis in his time in the lands he visited.

Another book which I have come upon is: "The Search for Atlantis, Excursions of a Layman Among Old Legends and New Discoveries," by Edwin Bjorkman. From it I learn that researches that are being made under the direction of Professor Adolf Schulten, have established that there was in Spain an "Hesperian counterpart to the ancient cultural centres of the orient." It was Tartessus, a city which was connected with Tyre in the east. The Scheria of Homer and the Atlantis of Plato can be identified with this cultural centre—so I learn from this brilliant and readable popularization of the results of Professor Schulten's researches. But Tartessus wasn't overwhelmed; it just decayed. Afterwards, in the interest of their trading monopoly, the Carthaginians closed the Atlantic routes against their Mediterranean rivals. Then they gave out that the famous city that had traded with Tyre had been overwhelmed by the terrible outer ocean. The story of Atlantis was a by-product of propaganda the object of which was the terrorization of adventurers with mercantile ambitions. If we want to raise objection to an origin of this kind for the legend, we can do so, I think, on a ground exactly opposite to that which may be taken against Lewis Spence's argument: the time allowed for the creation of the legend is too short: from the closing of the Atlantic trade-routes by the Carthaginians to Plato's time was only about one hundred years, and it is difficult to believe that a legend of great note could be built up in such a space of time.

Lewis Spence brings a great deal of testimony to show that the earliest people in Europe who were capable of creating a civilization—the Cro-Magnon, the Magdalenian, the Azilian-Tardenosian men—had their first appearance in Biscay and the Pyrenees: "Why, it may well be asked, should all these races appear suddenly in the same area?" The answer that he makes is that they were all colonists from a disintegrating Atlantis, bringing with them the Atlantean culture in its various stages. That answer may be the right one. But I have been led to read about discoveries in the Sahara that indicate that the part of Africa near the Pyrenees was the scene of human activities hundreds of centuries before the appearance of the Cro-Magnons in Southern France. This seems to signify that the earliest people in Europe capable of creating a civilization came overland, not oversea: the desert, then, and not the ocean may cover our earliest fatherland. Turn we now to the Pacific.

A Half-Day's Ride or Estates in Corsica

Easter Island is at once a riddle and a key to a riddle, and so Professor Macmillan Brown names his book "The Riddle of the Pacific." Part of the riddle of Easter Island is known even to those who take little interest in the problems of Polynesia. On the island, ringing it around, are great statues; they have been overthrown since the European discovery of the island, and they are now prone on the ground. It is true that these statues (we can look on two of them at the entrance to the British Museum; very uncouth pieces of workmanship they are) were made out of material that is easily worked; it did not require many workers nor a great deal of time to cut out in a crater-workshop even one of the statues that weighed thirty tons. But it did require a great many workers to transport them from the extinct volcano where they had been cut out, and to set up the platforms of cut stone that are associated with the statues. It is impossible, according to Professor Macmillan Brown, to think of Easter Island as ever producing food enough to suffice for a population adequate to the work of moving the statues. Moreover, the beams and rollers by which they might have transported them could not have been obtained on the island—there are no forests and there never were any forests there. And the present population of Easter Island gives no evidence that it ever possessed enough directive ability to carry out such a work as the cutting-out, the transporting, and the setting up of these large-sized images.

Who put up the statues, and why were they put up?

Strange Nostalgia

What relation have they, Polynesian as they are in the type they represent, to the present Polynesian population of Easter Island? And what bearing have the statues on the problems connected with Polynesian culture and the Polynesian dispersal through the islands of the Pacific?

To the east of Easter Island, Professor Macmillan Brown declares, was an archipelago known in Easter Island tradition as Motu Matiro Hiva; to the west there were islands known as Marae Renga and Marae Toiho. The archipelago and the two islands have gone down. In "The Riddle of the Pacific" he puts forward the lost Motu Matiro Hiva as the seat of a Polynesian Empire. The archipelago had wealth, organization, a subject population; its rulers resolved to make the barren place that we now know as Easter Island the cemetery for their conspicuous dead. They landed a slave-population on the place, and they kept them in subjection by controlling the food supplies, which were not grown on but brought to the island. The Empire-makers with their control of slave-labour had the statues cut out and put up; they were, according to Professor Macmillan Brown, arranging great avenues of statues and raising great platforms when the catastrophe came upon their own land. On Easter Island the population downed tools, and since that time never achieved any discipline or any real social order.

His contribution to the elucidation of the riddle presented by Easter Island lies in his analysis of the social order—or lack of social order—there, and its departures

A Half-Day's Ride or Estates in Corsica

in culture from the Polynesian norm. He makes a case
for his picturesque theory of a Polynesian Empire in
the southern temperate zone. He spoils it from time to
time, I think, by pressing too hard upon scraps of evidence. For instance, Easter Islanders call their little
speck of land Te Pito te Henua which means "The
Navel of the World." That seems testimony to the
theory that it had an archipelago and islands around it.
But then I remember that the Hawaiians call their volcano by just the same name—Ka Piko o Ka Honua. As
there were no lands surrounding the Hawaiian group,
the title cannot imply there what Professor Macmillan
Brown thinks it implies for Easter Island—a centre of
lands. And in order to make it credible that great labours
should go to the making of the island into a cemetery,
he has to declare that the men of Motu Matiro Hiva
were an ancestor-worshipping people. There is no war-
rant in Polynesian tradition for maintaining this. The
Polynesian stories, the Polynesian customs, the Polynesian myths do not give the impression that the Pacific
islanders were ancestor-worshippers. We know that
their great reverence was not for ancestors, but for the
Areiki, the *Alii*, the "Divine Ones," "The Heaven-
born," the living chiefs and kings who had the power
of *tapu*. In Hawaii the bones of the great kings, instead
of being marked, were carefully hidden away, and there
is always in the stories a devoted attendant who carries
out this duty. The secret of where the great Kamehameha is laid is still carefully preserved. . . .

"Hawaiki," they say on every island from New Zea-

Strange Nostalgia

land to Hawaii, naming the land their fathers came from. But was Hawaiki the Motu Matiro Hiva of Easter Island tradition, and is this homeland another Atlantis, lost beneath the waves?

EPIC OF THE SEA AND EPIC OF THE DESERT

OF EPICS in the sense of compositions that have a far-reaching theme, a high and singular style, a multiplicity of interest, a tragic and heroic outlook, I can think of two that have been written in modern days: one ostensibly a novel and the other ostensibly a record of travel—"Moby Dick" and "Travels in Arabia Deserta."

On the surface Melville's book is a novel: it is a prose narrative of a certain length dealing with possible men and possible events. But below the surface it is different. The men are possible, but they are also fabulous. The prose loosens into extraordinary rhythms. The event is possible, but it is also unique—it is nothing less than the pursuit of "the mightiest animated mass that has survived the flood." What Herman Melville proposes to himself is a theme not for a novel but for an epic.

His characters are generalized like the characters of an epic—"Ahab" and "Ishmael" are names that rule out merely personal characteristics. Captain Ahab is an Achilles of the sea. There is hardly any character in the story; the incidents are only rehearsals for the great central incident—the conflict between the steel-hearted man and the strange whale that comes to represent "the mightiest animated mass that has survived the flood." If Melville had consciously proposed to himself to make an epic of man's invasion of the oceans, his theme and his handling of it could hardly, it seems to me, be different. He is constantly striving to find a prose that can rise above the prose of mere narrative. Occasionally this prose is conventionally epical as when he has the Tahitian sailor speak the language of MacPherson's Ossian—

Hail, holy nakedness of our dancing girls! The Heeva-heeva! Ah, low-veiled, high-palmed Tahiti! I will rest on thy mat, but the soft soil has slid! I saw thee woven in the wood, my mat! Green the first day I brought you hence, now worn and wilted quite. Ah me! Not thou nor I can bear the change! How then, if so be transplanted to yon sky! Hear I the roaring streams from Pirohitee's peak of spears, when they leap down the crags and drown the villages? The blast! The blast! Up, spine, and meet it! [1]

"No fairy fingers can have pressed the gold, but devil's claws must have left their moulding there since yesterday," mutters the mate Starbuck, as he looks upon the doubloon that has been nailed to the mast as the reward for him who first catches sight of the white whale. Here the rhythmed speech that Melville rises to so often becomes regular blank verse—

[1] Compare "Age is on my tongue, my soul has failed. . . . I hear the call of years. They say as they pass along, why does Ossian sing? Soon shall he lie in the narrow house and no bard shall raise his fame! Roll on, ye dark-browed years; ye bring no joy in your course! Let the tomb open to Ossian for his strength has failed. The sons of song are gone to rest. My voice remains like a blast that roars lonely on a sea-surrounded rock after the winds are laid."

A Half-Day's Ride or Estates in Corsica

No fairy fingers can have pressed the gold
But devil's claws must have left their moulding there
Since yesterday.

In striving for this rhythmed prose, Melville—one notes with interest—comes again and again close to forms that one would think were exclusively of our day—free verse and polyphonic prose. Here is an example of his polyphonic prose—

It was a terrific, most pitiable, and maddening sight. The whale was now going head out, and sending his spout before him in a continual tormented jet; while his one poor fin beat his side in an agony of fright. Now to this hand, now to that, he yawed in faltering flight, and still at every billow that he broke, he spasmodically sank in the sea, or sideways rolled towards the sky his one beating fin.

This is in Chapter LXXXI. In Chapter LXX there is Captain Ahab's address to the whale's emptied head which has a polyphonic ring in it, although in this passage it is the assonance and not the rhyme that strikes on one's ear—

When unrecorded names and navies rust, and untold hopes and anchors rot; where in her murderous *hold* the frigate earth is ballasted with *bones* of millions of the drowned; there, in that awful water-land, there was thy most familiar *home*. Thou hast been where bell or diver never went; hast slept by many a sailor's *side* where sleepless mothers would give their *lives* to lay them *down*.

There is another passage (Chapter CII) which, without rhymes, approaches polyphonic prose—

Epic of the Sea and Epic of the Desert

The wood was green as mosses of the Icy Glen; the trees stood high and haughty, feeling their living sap; the industrious earth beneath was as a weaver's loom, with gorgeous carpet on it, where of the ground-vine tendrils formed the warp and woof, and the living flowers the figures. All the trees, with all their laden branches; all the shrubs and ferns and grasses; the message-carrying air; all these unceasingly were active. Through the lacings of the leaves, the great sun seemed a flying shuttle weaving the unwearied verdure. Oh, busy weaver! Unseen weaver! pause! one word! whither flows the fabric? What palace may it deck? Wherefore all these ceaseless toilings? Speak, weaver! Stay thy hand! But one single word with thee! Nay—the shuttle flies—the figures float from forth the loom; the freshet-rushing carpet forever slides away . . . Now amid the green, life-restless loom of that Arsacidean wood, the great, white, worshipped skeleton lay lounging—a gigantic idler! Yet, as the ever-woven verdant warp and woof intermixed and hummed around him, the mighty idler seemed the cunning weaver; himself all woven over with the vines; every month assuming greener, fresher verdure; but himself a skeleton. Life folded Death; Death trellised Life; the grim god wived with youthful Life, and begat him curly-headed glories.

There is an example of free verse in the foot-note to Chapter XLII. I take the liberty of presenting it as a separate poem—

THE ALBATROSS

I remember the first Albatross I ever saw. It was during a prolonged gale, in waters hard upon the Antarctic seas.
From my forenoon watch below, I ascended to the overclouded
deck; and there, dashed upon the main hatches I saw

A Half-Day's Ride or Estates in Corsica

A regal, feathery thing of unspotted whiteness, and with a
hooked, Roman bill sublime. At intervals

It arched forth its vast archangel wings, as if to embrace some
holy ark. Wondrous flutterings and throbbings shook it.

Though bodily unharmed, it uttered cries, as if some king's ghost
in supernatural distress. Through its inexpressible, strange
eyes,

Methought I peeped to secrets which took hold of God.

As Abraham before the angels I bowed myself; the white thing
was so white, and in those forever exiled waters I had lost
the miserable warping memories of traditions and of towns.

Long I gazed at that prodigy of plumage. I cannot tell, can
only hint the things that darted through me then. But at last
I awoke; and turning, asked a sailor what bird was this. A
goney, he replied.

Goney! I had never heard that name before; is it conceivable
that this glorious thing is utterly unknown to men ashore!
Never. But some time after I learned that goney was some
seaman's name for Albatross. . . .

But how has this mystic thing been caught? Whisper it not,
and I will tell; with treacherous hook and line, as the fowl
floated on the sea.

At last the Captain made a postman of it; tying a lettered,
leathern tally round its neck, with the ship's name and place;
and then letting it escape. But I doubt not, that leathern tally,
meant for man, was taken off in Heaven, when the white fowl
flew to join the wing-enfolding, the invoking, the adoring
Cherubim!

There is something tentative and experimental in the
language of this epic of the sea. Nothing of the kind is
in the language of the epic of the desert, for Charles
Doughty writes as if a great epic speech was natural to
him. And yet the possession of such a medium must rep-

resent a conquest. A disciple, as he describes himself, "of the divine Muse of Spenser and Venerable Chaucer," he was better prepared than Melville was to obtain the mastery over a great and appropriate idiom. He carried into the desert with him, fifty years ago, the spaciousness of Chaucer and Spenser, and an English, we must believe, that had a pristine freshness; he came out of the desert with a book that is no less a monument of language than it is a record of travel. The English of "Travels in Arabia Deserta" is of an amazing copiousness and an extraordinary dignity; he has grafted on to its seventeenth-century vigor a thorny Arabic growth—names of things common in the desert.

But in spite of this Arabic grafting, in spite of its archaic words and odd locutions, Doughty's English remains in the mind, not as words written, but as words said. All through the thousand pages of the volumes we have a sense of speech. Open "Travels in Arabia Deserta" at any page and you will hear a man talking—

The poor gleeman, chopfallen, and hollow with hunger, sat down wearily, of late he had found no more to eat than a cricket; all this week, he told us, there had passed through his gullet no more than the smoke of a little tittun, and water. The sheykhs now returning, "Alas!" said he, "and is it thus the Moahib deal with their guests? I die, and ye shall bury me here in Shellal; for wellah I may never have strength to go from hence, except I set out to-morrow,—and I had departed before, but was in dread to be met with by some of the Fukara." The Arab hearing his sorrowful complaint, sat silent: then Tollog said kindly, "O Aly, we are sorry for thee, but seest thou into what straitness we be fallen ourselves:" an ungenerous word was not cast in his

teeth, for that were against the reverence of God's hospitality.
—The Beduins willingly plead for each other, and one will make
a vaunt for another, but it is at the cost of breath, saying (that
biblical sentence) "He is better than I," so Hamed had praised
his poet to me, that I might bestow upon him fever medicines.

Compare with this, or with any passage of Doughty's,
this passage or any passage out of Colonel Lawrence's
introduction to the book—

Each tribe has its district in the desert. The extent and nature of these tribal districts are determined by the economic
laws of camel-breeding. Each holds a fair choice of pasture all
the year round in every normal year, and each holds enough
drinking water to suffice all its households every year; but the
poverty of the country forces an internal subdivision of itself
upon the tribes—

and you have all the difference between what is written
and what is uttered. The spell of desert Arabia is in
the voice that we hear continuously—a voice that has
got the wilderness into it—something brooding and of
another world. And it conveys a life as old as the oldest
written history. To say that Doughty's book gives the
soul of the people is to say less than the truth: it gives
the soul and the body, the garb and the odour of the
Semite of the desert.

What is in these volumes is gossip, but gossip of an
epical kind: it is as if a man with an enormous receptivity
began to talk to us about a neighbourhood, and kept up
his talk day after day and week after week. But the
neighbourhood that this man talks into existence is

Epic of the Sea and Epic of the Desert

"the huge and mostly waste Arabian Peninsula," with its tribes that are at once the grandest and the most abject of human beings, the Semites of the desert who "are like to a man sitting in a cloaca to his eyes, and whose brows touch heaven." And what epical speech he has found to give us this epical gossip in—

The man was Said, a personage of African blood, one of the libertines of the emir's household. He sat before us with that countenance and stiff neck, which by his estimation should magnify his office: he was lieutenant of the lord of the land's dignity in these parts. Spoke there any man to him, with the homely Arabian grace *ya Said!* he affecting not to look again, seemed to stare in the air, casting eyes over your head and making merchants' ears, bye and bye to awaken, with displeasure, after a mighty pause: when he questioned any himself he turned his back, and coldly averting his head he feigned not to attend your answer.

No Westerner could have been less of a Semite than this man who went into desert Arabia alone, and went wandering from tribe to tribe, and from hair-booth to hair-booth. "The sun," he says, "made me an Arab, but never warped me into Orientalism." He was an Englishman of the heroic and simple kind, and he remained an Englishman although he took on the endurance of an Arab of the desert. All that he has recorded is, as he says, "the seeing of a hungry man and the telling of a most weary man." But it is his continuous hunger and his long-drawn weariness that helped him to make us realize that "huge and mostly waste Arabian Peninsula," where a morsel of bread and salt eaten with another becomes a sacrament. I know of no other writer who has been able to place, as Doughty has placed, a whole society in a book. For it is a society that he gives us—that ancient society out of which have come the prophets and the great creeds. If it is not the strangest society that is upon the earth it is certainly the most tragic society. Men and women roam over a vast infecundity, hungry always, sleepless with the cold at night, smitten by the sun in the daytime. And they are tragic, not because of the physical hardships they endure—the American Indians endured hardships as great—but because these hungry and barely-clad wanderers have united themselves to a dream that is the loftiest, the most consistent, the least humanly-indulgent of human dreams. Doughty moves through this society, sharing its hunger, its cold, and its burning marches, its languors and its great loneliness, knowing its great men and its kindly men, its wastrels and its witless ones. Sometimes he sees them as the worst of all the children of Adam; sometimes he sees them as all but the noblest of men. He puts both judgments down, leaving us to reconcile them. "Travels in Arabia Deserta" is an heroic book—heroic in its length, heroic in the very language that it is written in, a book that has come out of an heroic endurance and that celebrates an heroic and tragic people. "What went ye out into the desert to see?" was asked of old. "A reed shaken in the wind? But what went ye out into the desert to see? A man clothed in soft garments? Behold, those who are clothed in soft garments are in the houses of Kings." Doughty went out into

Epic of the Sea and Epic of the Desert

the desert, and what he saw belongs to the desert—men hardened in an infecundity and of a high and brooding fantasy. He has told us of these men in the great speech that, as it seems, comes upon men in the desert.

BIRDS, BEASTS, AND PUPPETS

It is true what Yorick said: they order these things better in France. Against a background of bright-barred cages, moving birds, heaps of green, men and women move as if they were not in an everyday world. They are looking into cages, or holding them up with a kind of devoutness. A young woman looks into one she is carrying as if this bird was the last thing in the world she could bear to part from, and a battered old body peers longingly into a cage that a tough in velveteens holds out to her. Beside his heap of green stuff an ancient merchant who looks as if he had spent the night in the fields is counting his francs into a pouch, and kindly-looking as Baucis and Philemon, an old couple are dispensing seeds from their little stall.

It is the Bird Market of Paris on a Sunday forenoon. Sparrows on the pavement pick up seeds scattered from the cages or shaken out of bags that purchasers are taking home. Sunday morning must be a grand time for the sparrows hereabouts; they are able to pick up seeds not intended for their consumption; they must feel like gamins used to stale crusts who come upon bags of buns. The little birds in the cages show no resentment against the sparrows, no envy of their enlargement: they are tiny birds, drab but for a stain of red upon their breasts and tiny beaks: a score of them roost upon long perches; they hate to be at the end of a perch, and the couple that get there flutter into the middle of their fellows and crash into new places. These birds are bought, I presume, by young men for rather wild young ladies. They perch on the finger-tip or nestle at the breast like Lesbia's sparrow. And then, like Lesbia's sparrow, they die—just because Lesbia has to think about something else.

The street of the canaries is more lively than the street of the love-birds. Here are canaries of all shades of yellow—your daffodil-yellow, your orange-tawny, your laburnum-yellow, your gosling-green. Here, too, are canaries blanched and canaries tufted and ruffled. Here are canary-linnets and canary-finches. Men, holding cages in their hands, are comparing canaries with fine virtuosity: they are their sonnets, their rondels, their sestinas, their chants-royal. Near by are little birds that seem to have drawn into their brown feathers a colour from the setting sun: flame-finches; and birds that are red-headed and wild-crested, and birds that look like enamelled starlings. I hear the word "Madagascar" and I go to see the birds that have come from that island of Malays and negroes, of ostriches and crocodiles. But they are neither very colourful nor very lively. The woman has others. She has dishevelled hair, this woman, two teeth are in her gums, and she wears long ear-rings. The breeding and rearing of parakeets is an hereditary profession with her; generations of her family have engaged themselves in it, and what I am being shown now is the fine flower of parakeetry. Never were well-coloured birds so shapely as these, and never were shapely birds so well-coloured. There are ten in a cage, and there seems to be room for all, and all seem to be in good-fellowship. Indeed, these parakeets seem to know that, sitting in line, they make a perfect decoration: green breast after green breast, and, in the middle, a back barred with yellow, tapering down into a tail that has in it the blue that kingfishers affect—a blue that any kingfisher might be proud of. They are being sold in dozens and pairs, and the woman with the long ear-rings can relate histories of them all.

Pigeons, comparatively enormous, are in crates: canary cages are on top of the crates, and the pigeons seem to be taking credit for the canaries' singing, so complacent are they. A white, unstirring one is in a cage that is just a size larger than it is, and a woman with a black shawl across her shoulders, under a black umbrella, is seated beside it. On the pavement beside her are sacks of fresh greens—chickweed and groundsel—and people are buying them from her in handfuls. Everything that can give comfort and even distraction to a bird is displayed. There are bundles of cane for the making of perches, woven foundations for nests, sacks and sacks of every kind of seed, imitation tree-trunks with green imitation mosses on them and a hole through which a bird can get into a hollow. There are fish-shaped bones (they are skeletons of cuttle-fish) for birds to sharpen their beaks on, and tinsel-bright balls to hang in cages—all sorts of far-brought, surprising things to make birds forget their forests and fields.

Birds, Beasts, and Puppets

And in the middle of the market, sitting most trust-ingly in an open basket, is a cat—she is for sale. A Siamese cat, an appealing cat, a pet of a cat! She is small like a Cambodian princess. She has little pointed ears, well-defined and neat whiskers, and a soft, soft tail. Her eyes are pieces of perfect jade. Cats when they are at ease radiate complacency, self-satisfaction. Not this princess. Something different, something, I know not what, radiates from her. If a toy could be-come alive for a favourite child it would radiate what comes from this cat—an enchantment that would be continuous. And here she is in the Bird Market with a scarlet ribbon round her neck, for sale, and her price is not fifty thousand, but just fifty francs.

They order these things better in France; still, in London there is a Bird-and-Beast Shop that always holds me. Over it a Roman peace broods. Rabbits rest beside dogs, and doves doze beside a wide-eyed kestrel. Canary cages hang outside the shop: their interiors are painted blue, and each inmate is of a different shade of yellow. A squirrel is in his woodland browns, and beside him, in metallic greens, a parrot—an old, hashish-sleepy parrot. White cockatoos lean towards one another in at-titudes borrowed from pigeons: they would be the very representatives of loving couples were it not that their eyes are hard and old. Next them are the pigeons. Hu-man communications have corrupted them; at opposite sides of their cage they sit, each meditating on the enormous bust it has attained to. But the little doves have still the quickness of the wild; they fly around their cages, and their heads have the lightness of the heads of larks.

At one window there are enormous cages: all around the interiors mice are stuck like dead things. Did some butcher-bird get loose in the night and impale them all? But they are not dead, these mice; like infinitesimal monkeys they cling to the bars of the cages. Their claws are powerful, and they have jewels for eyes. Three cages swarm with these mealy-colored mice. And in a fourth cage a single delicately colored mouse appears.

These brown, swarming mice recall the meadows and the movement of summer. The creatures neighbouring them are of the meadows also, but there is nothing about them that recalls life and movement: they are hedge-hogs; they lie in darkness like creatures that have bad dreams. Their breathing makes their bodies appear like the bodies of emaciated men. One of them lifts his snout and shows his rat's eyes, and the other pushes his head away. They hate the world and they hate each other; these hedgehogs are the very types of what is un-sociable. Then there are the guinea-pigs. We have con-founded in the same swinish nomenclature hedgehogs and guinea-pigs. But guinea-pigs are gregarious while hedgehogs are brutishly alone. Watch guinea-pigs eat together; their heads and ears move as they munch; they crowd like ladies round a bargain-counter. These guinea-pigs have adopted rabbits into their tribe; when the rabbits are quiet they lie with their heads against their furs, when the rabbits move they make perpetual movement with them.

Birds, Beasts, and Puppets

Just outside the door of the shop there is a cage with a magpie in it. This magpie can whistle and say "hillo," but his accomplishment has made him socially difficult. He sits sulky and apart, like a neglected actor in a public-house. And now, delicately, a white rat comes to the edge of his cage and looks out with wavering eyes. The tortoise in the cage that is just over him has folded his forepaws inward precisely like a woman resting with her arms akimbo; his eyes have the limpidness of a philosopher's who has discovered and taken his elixir. Perhaps he knows that he, the tortoise, gives the elements of repose and durability to the establishment. Intimacy is supplied by the Persian cat who now steps out through the house-door. She rubs herself against the human beings and nods familiarly to those in the cages. "How do, creatures," she seems to say. "Nice day, isn't it? I can't stay long. I've such a lot of people to see to-day. Tiresome, isn't it?" The puppies in the cages are astonished. The kittens cease playing around and look at her. A rabbit sits up and makes round, foolish eyes. The cat does not stay; she turns back into the house and marches upstairs.

And I, as I turn round, hear a squeaking utterance that is familiar. Is it from a cockatoo, or from a monkey? The squeaking utterance has exciting associations. And then I see the narrow booth, the violent figures before the little opening, and the big disillusioned dog that sits apart. It is the Punch and Judy Show. "Well, sir, if you found him three weeks ago, sir, that proves, sir, that the little dog is mine, sir." The dog-owner's is plain speech. The utterance of Punch is a staccato of squeaks. Master Punch, as the most venerable character in the puppet-comedy, preserves the hieratic speech. I turn up the collar of my coat and fall into the youngster's expectant attitude. The promenading sandwich-men stop for a minute; the belted messenger-boys cease to be sharp-eyed and become round-eyed. This puppet-play gains a real audience, for nothing is so pleasing to the sons of men as the spectacle of triumphant self-assertion, and this is what we are being given. But Punch, at last, meets his end, and is seen no more in the opening of the booth. Tired and stiff, Toby, the little dog, jumps down on the pavement, accepting the fact that a move has to be made to another stand. Already the booth is being wheeled off on a barrow. And a cat, a white cat that looks thoroughly domesticated, is now seated upon it.

As I left the Bird Market I heard a call that had a sharp edge to it. And then, alert, independent, nonchalant, seven goats came towards me along the boulevard. A long-backed black dog with a curly tail turned them, and the goats crossed the thoroughfare.

As they crossed they bunched together; then, having reached the sidewalk, they strung themselves out, each goat going her own gait. Some were hornless, some had little horns, some had little tassels from their necks, and all were as sleek as fawns. They were able to go with good speed on their little hoofs, but they liked to make this a promenade. The solemn dog with the curly tail kept close to them, but they did not allow themselves to be disturbed by his attentions. A man with a black box

[191]

upon his back and carrying a long-lashed, brass-bound whip, went with them. The long lash of the whip sometimes gave the goats direction. Sometimes the man leant on the whip and discussed the price of goat-cheese— packages of it were in his black box. Sometimes, after he and the dog had given them direction, the seven saw a clear way ahead of them, and then they went on a ramble after their own hearts. The man would put his little pipe to his mouth and blow the call that has the queer sharp edge to it—the call that knife-grinders in Spain make. The call went down the street: a woman came out to buy goats' milk, and the one to be milked stood patiently—patiently, but with roving eyes. The others waited. Then they swiftly strung themselves out and went down the boulevard, creatures that, knowing themselves to be tameless, need show no resentment nor any sign of broken spirit. Unlike cattle, unlike sheep, they make every way they go their own whimsical, roving way.

The call with the sharp edge to it brought another out on the street. This time cheese was bargained for. The goats made a circle around a tree on the sidewalk; they bit off little bits of the bark. One of them turned her attention to a notice pasted on a wall: raising herself a little on her hind legs she nipped off bits of it and ate them with great gusto. The lash went forth; Curly Tail crowded up; the little herd moved on. And then a black cat came out on the pavement; she tasted a morsel of the cheese dropped by her mistress, and looked after them as the seven goats went down the street.

A MEDITATION ON CAKES

WHAT is this, I say to myself, as, seated on an un-
charged-for bench in the Luxembourg Gardens, I perceive faint smoke go up beside near-by trees. A tall,
grey woman is beside where the smoke ascends; before
her is a square, soot-black structure, and I can see that
she has a ladle in her hand. Some priestess of a rite that
has to be performed on a black altar in the open air,
I permit myself to imagine. I look more intently on
the scene. A string of people are before the altar-like
structure, each with the peculiar intentness of those
who are in expectation of some benefit: I watch the sibyl
handing each a honey-coloured cake. Thereupon I approach the soot-black structure myself. The sibyl takes
pieces of charcoal and puts them on a fire that is within
the black square. Beside her is a great can of creamy
paste. She takes up a ladleful: pulling out a pan she
pours it in; she presses a cover down upon the paste,
twists the pan upside down, and deftly pushes it within
what is, after all, an oven set amongst trees. She draws it
back in a minute; there, with diamond-like punches upon
it, is an oblong cake. Shaking sugar on it she hands the
cake to the first in line. It is a commercial transaction, I
discover: there is an announcement "Gaufres, 80 cen-
times." And now I stand in line to receive one, with a

soldier who wears a fez, a child who holds a toy-balloon, an old harridan, a very chic lady, and a man wearing velveteen trousers, a muffler and a cap, with an empty sack hanging across his shoulder, who nevertheless looks like an artist, and who (as I was to learn) supports a large family by collecting and marketing ants' eggs. I receive my gaufre. It is one of those cakes that are puffed into layers of paste; it is very tasty. I discover that it is rather like the American waffle, and am led to guess that "waffle" and "gaufre" are cognate words.

Back on my bench I can think of nothing else than cakes; my stream of consciousness flows around cakes. It is Shrove Tuesday, the eve of Lent. It has always been recognized that the most satisfactory way of preparing for a fast is to have a feast. The best part of a feast, it has always seemed to me, is the part in which cakes have a place; a feast in which no time is wasted getting to the cakes—in which the cakes constitute the feast—is the best of feasts. Pancake Night, Shrove Tuesday, as I discern now, is rightly placed before Ash Wednesday: the happiest feast before the longest fast.

It is true that the cakes eaten on this feast are cakes in their simplest form—to wit, pancakes. But pancakes made by a practised pancake-maker (and there are, the Lord be praised, many such!) make a dish fit for a better man than a king—a dish fit for a sage. When I think of sages eating pancakes, I think of them as eating pancakes made thin and with much butter on their surfaces. As a youth I used to tramp from house to house in a certain district in Ireland on Shrove Tuesday evening.

A Half-Day's Ride or Estates in Corsica

I had forty aunts (well, not quite forty) all adepts in pancake-making, and all living conveniently near to one another. I managed to visit nearly every one of them on Pancake Night.

The best story I ever read has the making of pancakes for its central incident. You will find it in the Thousand and One Nights; not in any of the abbreviated versions; it is somewhere in Burton's seventeen volumes, or if not in Burton, in Payne, or if not in Burton or Payne, in Monsieur Mardrus's French version. It is entitled "The Caliph and the Daughter of Kisra." The central incident, the luminous point which, as Robert Louis Stevenson tells us, should be recognizable in every well-constructed story, is where the Daughter of Kisra is sent pancakes by the Caliph. They are in a silver dish and the Daughter of Kisra, with the generosity that characterized her royal house, has dish and pancakes sent to the young man who gave her a cruse of water when she was in need of refreshment in the streets of Bagdad. The silver dish is offered for sale in the market; the Caliph recognizes it, and this leads to very remarkable developments. It may not be the best story ever written, but it is the best instance I know of pattern in story-telling. And the central incident, as I have stated, is the making of the pancakes; they are made by the Caliph himself; Haroun al-Raschid tucks up his sleeves, makes the batter, pours it on the pan, holds it on the brazier, and repeats this over and over until the great silver dish is packed with pancakes. A most memorable incident, I maintain.

A Meditation on Cakes

I had a grandmother. I don't remember her pancakes, but I have a distinct memory of a special cake she used to make for me. This cake was named in Irish "Keestha Bosca," which means "the cake of the palm"; it had this name because it was shaped in the palm of the maker out of dough left over from baking the bread for next day. In my grandmother's house (this is a long time ago and things have changed since) most of the bread we ate was baked in the pot-oven at night. Probably the mixing and the kneading and the putting of the dough into the oven took place at no great length of time after candle-light. But to a child lying in bed and keeping awake to watch such proceedings they seemed to be at a very remote time in the night. My grand-mother's bread was mixed in buttermilk and with soda. When it was put in the oven, the coals and ashes of a turf-fire were put around the oven and over it. And on the lid of the pot was placed "the cake of the palm," after sugar and sweet milk had been placed on the top of it.

I have never lost my taste for cakes. After the cakes of folk-culture such as pancakes and "the cake of the palm," came cakes that were still popular but approaching the cakes of higher cultivation: squares of ginger-bread sold off carts at little fairs or in little shops; ginger-cakes which were very vitalizing as one faced a mile of road on a chill evening (in those remote days one could get a bagful for twopence). Later on there was a heavy, clammy cake that one bought in pennyworths—Chester-cake it was called. It was related that the ingredients

of this cake were always mixed in beer—in porter—
and this rumour added to the worth of the cake, to our
minds, by giving it a dark and secret origin. And, still
on the border between the cakes of folk-culture and the
cakes of higher cultivation, there were spiced cakes and
cream tarts.

Then came cakes of the higher cultivation—cakes
with icings, cakes with rare fruits crowning them and
embedded in them, cakes that are the creations of medi-
tative and daring intelligences. All such cakes are a
temptation to me—all, I should say, except cakes that
have chocolate outside or inside of them. I think such
cakes are mistakes. I see people whose tastes I know
to be indisputable eating them, and it is as if I saw them
reading the longer poems of Dante Gabriel Rossetti.
Chocolate cakes are not for me.

I do not know what ingredients should go into a cake,
nor how the ingredients should be combined, nor how
the combination should be baked. But I know the temper in which cakes should be made. The temper should
be that of affection and light-heartedness. Soups can
be made by slaves. Meats may be cooked by mockers
and salads mixed by suspicious, cross-eyed servitors.
Fish and fowl can be prepared by fleshly men sunk in
infamies. But cakes can only be made by the candid.
Everyone knows that Cinderella could make cakes and
that her jealous half-sisters couldn't, and it is clear to
Shakespearean scholars that Cordelia was a cake-maker.
"I offer you cakes and friendship," said a remarkable
lady to me once. She, being the most experienced lady

A Meditation on Cakes

in Dublin, knew that these two went together. I cherish
her friendship still and have happy memories of her
cakes. And I know a lady in Chicago whose cakes (or
should I call them cates?) are the sort that the Queen of
Sheba gave Solomon when full of friendship for him.

I remember that there used to be a cake-maker in this
quarter who made cakes in his own little stall. He was
a Constantinopolitan; perhaps he made cakes as the
Caliph did, tucking up his sleeves and holding the pan
above the brazier. But I could not recall his method
and was teased into going in search of his stall. Three
little shops were together: I remembered them; the
first sold firewood and had, as is the pleasant fashion in
Paris, logs painted all over its front, the round ends
showing notches and the grain: intended to be repre-
sentational, this shining pattern of logs was so stylized
as to be symbolic, evoking the lives of wood-cutters
dwelling in huts in château-surrounding forests. Almost touching upon this shop was another outside of
which were hanging three deep, richly-glowing copper
basins. The Constantinopolitan's was between the two.
The stall was small and bare: there was in it room for
the stove, the kneading-board, the cauldron of oil, and
the cake-maker himself. At the back was an unremark-
able curtain, behind which, no doubt, birds sang, and
fountains played, and odalisques awaited their master.
I ordered a couple of his cakes. He punched out a circle
in the dough on his kneading-board, and punched a hole
in that circle of dough; then he plunged the piece into
the cauldron of boiling oil. He took it out, crisp and

swollen, oily, ring-shaped, and golden-brown. He made another and put the couple in paper for me. They were the sort that is known in America as doughnuts, and were admirable of their kind.

A CASUAL ONLOOKER

THE nicest thing about Paris, as a friend remarked to me the other day, is the number of perfectly natural things one is always coming upon. I do not include amongst such natural things the spectacle of ostriches drawing light vehicles down a main thoroughfare. I have come upon it, but with more surprise than entertainment. With ostriches I have only an imperfect sympathy: they are at once light-headed and heavy-footed; that knot on the top of their neck which is their head must leave them practically brainless. Still, the sight of these particular ones stripped of their plumes (the one distinction an ostrich possesses), with their backs bare, and being forced to do something they couldn't possibly see any reason in, made me feel that they were rather unfortunate. I was glad to perceive that the experiment of attaching ostriches to vehicles and driving down the Boulevard du Montparnasse was not apt to succeed. You can't really bridle an ostrich; you can fasten a rein somewhere about his beak, but you can't guide him with it, for the reason that it doesn't control his neck; that neck is not a fixed thing; it's like a piece of string that can bend backwards and forwards, sideways, and up and down; a rein can't force the animal in any particular direction. And so this tooling of ostriches will not become a regular sight, I prophesy.

Vendors with their various vehicles are amongst the natural sights of Paris that can entertain a casual on-looker like myself. I saw one of these vendors the other day in the most natural of postures. He was asleep upon, or rather against, his hand-cart—the vehicle be-ing on its shafts, his feet were on the ground. The hour was just after noontide, and the place he had picked on to repose himself was just to the right of the great scar-let doors of Notre Dame. He was an old man with a remarkable resemblance to Victor Hugo—I could note the resemblance although his cap was pulled down to shade his eyes from the sun. The pair of dogs that helped him to pull were at his feet in a slumber so profound that the proverb about letting sleeping dogs lie could not apply to them: they would lie no matter what one did to them; if ever I saw creatures slumber-bound they were these two lean dogs; now and again one or the other twitched a foot as if his dream was still con-cerned with padding the hard pavement. Pilgrims were going in through the scarlet doors, the city traffic was sweeping up and down, but still the old man slumbered against his hand-cart, immobile as the apostles in the façade of the cathedral, each of his dogs as supine as the dragon Saint Michael has pierced. He was like a picture of Vigour Reposing Itself. What was his mer-chandise? Rags and scrap-iron, and, as it seemed to me, pieces of string. Pieces of string were knotted to every corner of his cart; his dogs' harness was tied with pieces of string, and his boots which had never formed a proper pair were stitched and laced with pieces of string; his clothes were tied with strings. I was not present at his awakening. When I got back to the place ten minutes after I had looked on him, he was gone with his cart and his dogs, and there wasn't even a piece of string left behind. I suppose he and his dogs could be awake and away quicker than any of us.

I had discovered that Paris is a city of noble-looking horses, but it was here, in the great place before Notre Dame, that I marked them and the vehicles they draw. The streets do not afford a real view of horse and vehicle; they are coming towards us or else going by us at too close range. But as I look across the front of the Cathedral I can view horses and vehicles as upon a magnificently prepared course. Here, upon a high pedestal is the bronze of a mounted king who holds a sceptre that is like an uplifted spear (Charlemagne, I suppose). They whirl past as though this statue were the pivot of their course, and from the side I sit the place is wide enough to afford a view of the spectacle. These vehicles are chariots. Here is one to which three horses are yoked, a chariot piled high with timbers. The horses that are together seem to be racing each other and straining desperately to gain upon the one that leads; their necks are arched, their manes are afloat; the charioteer upon his high seat makes the whip sound, and I doubt if the warrior-king ever looked upon a more heroic sight. Then another chariot piled with bright metal shavings whirls by; it has two horses; their hoofs strike the ground in splendid rhythm.

I spent the rest of the day taking note of the types of chariot that course through the streets and along the boulevards. They are very various. First and foremost is the long unenclosed chariot whose horses go with out-stretched necks as if to emphasize the lengthiness of the vehicle; the drivers on their level and seated rather far back. This particular type has high scarlet wheels—two wheels that are as high above as below the body—which give it a processional appearance; the drivers are covered with coal-dust and blackened bags hang on the rail behind as in celebration of some Plutonian triumph. Along the sides, painted in red on a semi-circle above the wheels is a name such as a demon might have— "Chaco," or else (in derision, I suppose) "Pantheon." Seen from behind, a string of these chariots is superbly processional: the high wheels gleam, the drivers, one before another, seem small and eager, their whips are held up like wands or sceptres. Then there are great closed chariots which are very high; they are drawn by horses on whose collars are great plates of brass and above the collars triangles of bells; these have two pairs of wheels, the front ones being lower than the hind ones; these chariots are filled with jars and bottles, and they go with speed and magnificent rhythm. As night came on I saw coming through the shades a chariot in-side of which hung carcasses of oxen. The charioteer was bare-armed, and above his corduroy was a vest of hide. He was bearded, but with the trim-beardedness of

a Roman, and his neck-cloth streamed each side of him.
His outcry was accompanied by lashing that was swish
and thud indeed. He shouted something to me, and if
I had remembered my Latin I should have known who
he was and what he would have said, for it seemed to me
that I dimly recognized him. Later, at midnight, I saw
a very curious chariot: it was like the top of a railway
engine mounted upon a flat vehicle; it was drawn by two
pairs of horses. Very high sat the driver; he was swathed
in capes and he held straight up a whip that was to the
height of the boulevard trees. Fire poured from the
back of this chariot and the driver's cry as his lash
reached to the foremost pair of horses was strident
through its hoarseness. The iron on their hoofs showed
as silver flashes as the horses took their course.

The horses are grey generally with a dark grain showing through their hide; sometimes I see a black or cream-
coloured horse between shafts that looks as fine as any
Arab steed. Everything about them shows that their
masters are equine-conscious: their manes and tails
have been combed and streaming forelocks have been
left them; their shoes are in shining order, their harness is studded with brass; often scarlet tassels hang
from under their manes and blue fleeces are across their
saddles; their great collars are often of scarlet or are
faced with brass (the scarlet collars add greatly to the
appearance of the great white horses); moreover, they
have been trained to arch their necks and to strike the
ground with measured beat.

One has to be awake at night or very early in the

A Half-Day's Ride or Estates in Corsica

morning to be attentive to the splendidly rhythmed beat of horses' hoofs on the cobbles or the asphalt pavement, a beat of hoofs which accompanied by the ringing of bells and the thud of whips orchestrates the street. The horses swing along, the iron striking the ground in perfect measure—one horse or a team of horses, two, three, or four. The rattle of the harness goes with the beat of hoofs; there is the swish and crack, and finally the thud of the lash; there is the cry that goes with the lashing—the hoarse and exultant cry of the pursuer which is the authentic cry of the charioteer. I would represent this sound as "ghi"—our "gee," I suppose, is an infantile pronunciation of this Ur-Sanskrit word.

Sometimes I hear a beat without bell, without jangle of harness, a rigorous beat, and I know that a black vehicle is going by, one drawn by the blackest of horses on which a black-clothed driver keeps to a settled beat without a swish of the whip. And I have stopped where the chariots have stopped and have watched the horses. I have seen how they hang their heads and bend their knees, and how sometimes one of them makes the gesture of lifting a head and rubbing another's neck. But this is only a momentary movement, and there is never any response to it. They stand emptied of all inspiration. At once they rouse themselves when the rein draws their heads. They lurch; they stumble; then all at once they are going at speed, their iron-shod hoofs beating the cobbles or the asphalt pavement in heroic and stern rhythm. What brave creatures they are, these horses of Lutetia!

A Casual Onlooker

They bring me to where there are riders (I have never seen more than two or three in a company) who, mounted on donkeys, with panniers of brown earthenware pots each side of them, pace through streets and avenues. These, I find, are also amongst the natural sights that are entertaining. They are low-sized and light-weighted as is proper for men who bestride donkeys. They wear corduroy pants, with blouses and caps, and they have the look of persons who have pushed into remote territory. Generally they walk beside their delicately-stepping little beasts, only a head higher than they. Or they stand, man and donkey, beside the array of pots upon a pavement. Trudging man and trudging donkey look the tiredest things in the world. Standing beside the pots they look the patientest of all living things. Yet I have seen a party of these men mounted behind their panniers go down the Champs Elysées in quite a frisky fashion. In fact, when last I saw such a party their leader was singing what seemed to me to be a wild song of the South. And no wonder he was doing so. He was on his way to Lyons, Avignon, Perpignan, Barcelona, Valence, Alicante, and Madrid, having been in Amsterdam and Brussels. How do I know this? Well, I didn't know it then but I know it now. In Toulouse, in a newspaper office, I see the photograph of the identical man, his pots at his feet, his cap on his head, his blouse on his torso, his corduroys on his legs, and his little donkey beside him, and under the photograph is written "*Antonio Perez y Vinagre, fabricant d'Alcaraza à Salvaterre de los Barros, province de Badajon (Es-*

A Half-Day's Ride or Estates in Corsica

pagne), *parti à pied de cette ville le 4 Mars dernier, passant par Madrid, Alicante, Barcelone, Perpignan, Avignon, Lyon, Colmar, Amsterdam, Bruxelles, Paris, vient d'arriver à Toulouse, retournant en Espagne."* Viva Don Antonio!

THE SAD SEQUEL TO PUSS IN BOOTS

HE WAITED for me, this strange cat, and when I opened the door he entered the garret with me. I lighted my candle. Meantime he had seated himself on a stool at my table. I saw that he was a long cat and that he had quite a broad back; not a highly-bred animal, I should have said, but a plebeian of great character.

He had a wrinkled brow and eyes that were quite extraordinary. I declare they were like pieces of jade become alive. They were mournful eyes. The imperative of misery was upon the creature and he communicated it to me.

There was nothing for it, I realized, but to share my supper with him. I put my milk and bread into two bowls, and left one at my visitor's side of the table. He gave me a look of acknowledgment. When he ate, it was like one who had a fast to break.

Towards the end he ate slowly, as one crumbles bread at a table preparatory to the opening of a conversation. Then he said:

"I have called upon you, not merely because you have a good heart, but because you are a man of letters. You can make the history of my misfortunes known to the world. I had intended to call on Monsieur Voltaire, but I am informed that he still stays with the King of

A Half-Day's Ride or Estates in Corsica

Prussia. My case will not wait. I am not now as robust as I once was, and I cannot delay making my testament.

"Without further preface or preamble, I shall declare who I am. I am no other than the Cat of the Marquis of Carabas."

"The Cat of the Marquis of Carabas!" I cried, "then you must know the Marquise."

At that the cat jumped off the stool and went pacing up and down my garret. "The Marquise," he said in a most sinister tone, "oh, yes, I know the Marquise."

"I was privileged to see the Marquise at the opera the other night," I cried, giving expression—I will acknowledge it—to one of my life's enthusiasms. "What magnificence of beauty! Her jewels were the talk of the assembly. The Envoy from the Sophy of Persia said that the star above her forehead was unique—his master has no such jewel in his collection. But then it is said that her husband has a great estate."

"Surely you have heard the history of the Marquis of Carabas," said the cat, seating himself upon the stool once more.

"Surely," I said.

"You speak," said he impatiently, "as if people did not read Perrault any more."

"The Marquis of Carabas," I said, "a younger son, was he not? Quite penniless. He had a cat . . ." Then I looked at my visitor with great attention. "Dear me," I said, "is it possible that you are the Cat of the Marquis of Carabas—the celebrated Puss-in-Boots?"

"I am that unhappy character," he cried, "the more

The Sad Sequel to Puss in Boots

unhappy in the fact that my name and exploits do not
spring to your mind at once. But can people really be
so unmindful of one of the most sensational happenings
in Society in our time? A happening, moreover, that
has been recorded by a writer who is not only great but
well-known."

"You allude to Monsieur Perrault," I said, not without a trace—I am now free to confess it— of mortifica-
tion. "You allude to Monsieur Perrault. But it has
been stated on quite good authority that Monsieur Perrault did not really write the histories that bear his
name. His son, a boy of six years, really composed
them."

"What does it matter?" cried the cat with a greater
show of impatience. "What do these questions matter?
You all know the gossip about a book, but how few people nowadays really know the contents of a book! I had
expected more from you."

"The whole history comes back to me," I said hastily.
"Pray forgive my remissness. You aided the penniless
young man. You caught partridge in your bag and you
brought them to the King. 'Presents from the Marquis
of Carabas,' you said, thereby winning the interest of
the King who was very fond of partridge. You went
with the King and his daughter in their carriage one day,
and when you came to the river you cried out, 'My lord,
the Marquis of Carabas, is drowning.' When the young
man, whom you had instructed to bathe in the river,
was drawn out by the King's lackeys, you pretended that
his clothing had been stolen. The King ordered some of

his company to lend him clothes. Dressed up in finery
he was presented to the King. With his handsome person, and in the fashionable clothes that he now wore,
he made such an impression upon her that the King's
daughter fell in love with him.

"As the carriage drove into the country, the King
would ask, whenever he would see a splendid castle or a
particularly fine estate, 'Whom does this belong to?'
And you always replied, 'To my lord, the Marquis of
Carabas.'

"As a matter of fact, all those splendid castles and
admirable manors belonged to an ogre. As the carriage
came near the most imposing of the castles, you sprang
out and went swiftly towards it. As you had guessed,
the ogre was at home. You engaged him in conversation. Ogres, like the rest of us, are not averse to talking
of themselves and their activities. You asked him if it
were true that he could change himself into something
colossal. He changed himself into an elephant, if I remember aright. Then you asked if he could change himself into something tiny—a mouse, you suggested. He
changed himself into a mouse. You sprang upon and
devoured the transformed ogre. When the carriage arrived you were ready to welcome the King and his
daughter into the castle of the Marquis of Carabas.
The estates had already been appraised by the King.
The betrothal of the Princess and the young Marquis
of Carabas followed without delay. She is certainly
the most beautiful, the most charming and the most
amiable woman in Europe."

The Sad Sequel to Puss in Boots

The head of my visitor remained bowed, and I felt he was thinking furiously. "He was inconsiderate, of course," he said, "like all young men, but I refuse to believe that he was bad at heart—at least, not until his character was broken down by the sort of life she compelled him to lead. I cannot say as much for her. She was brought up at court, and you know what that means.

"I was disrespectful to her, she said. All that she meant was that I did not leave the room when she entered. She complained that I was impertinent enough to pass her on the stairway. But is it not excusable to make some little demonstration of one's worth after one has been railed at before servants? The truth of the matter is that the Marquise never liked me. From the moment her husband introduced me to her as his benefactor she was ill-disposed towards me. Why that should have been I do not know. But I saw hatred in her smile when she said, 'This, I suppose, is the Mayor of the Palace.'

"I had not asked the Marquis to make any definite arrangements in regard to my entertainment in the castle. But he knew perfectly well that I had been looking forward to certain satisfactions. It is true that I was not used to pheasant for breakfast. But just because I was not used to pheasant I wanted it. And, anyway, pheasants abounded on the Marquis of Carabas' estates.

"I think it was in the third week that I was informed by the majordomo that I could have pheasant only twice a week. When I complained about this I was told that the spectacle of my eating pheasant had a demoralizing effect on the household. After this, the higher servants refused to wait upon me. I went to the Marquis, and he remonstrated with them, but in no very strong terms. He gave them the liberty to say in their impertinence that they had not been engaged to wait on cats.

"After this one of the scullions waited on me. Then I had to give up going into the courtyard where I used to sun myself. The Marquise had had a dovecot placed there, and it was alleged that my presence alarmed the doves.

"You spoke of her jewelry. I have reason, I may tell you, to resent her passion for precious stones. Would you believe that the Marquise listened to an impostor who assured her that my eyes were not fleshly, but were absolutely solid, and were gems of the first water? After that she permitted herself the criminal desire of wanting to possess one of my eyes—your beautiful, charming and amiable Marquise!"

I stared into my visitor's eyes and noted that they were strangely green and unchanging.

"The Marquis actually came to ask me to give one of my eyes to his wife," he resumed. "He said that I was a pensioner of the household and did not need so many organs as those who were engaged in earning a living. I was provided for, he said. Also he would have me believe that my eyesight was so powerful that a single eye such as I possessed was enough for any creature. I was exceedingly indignant. Then the Marquis entreated me. In the name of our long and unbroken friendship, he

asked me to give him one of my eyes for his wife. I refused to listen to this plea. Finally he demanded my
eye in the name of his wife, a princess of the blood royal.

"I was made so furious that I sprang at him. My
claws did him no damage, however. And yet, that evening, no supper was served me.

"Naturally I was resolved to have it out with the
Marquis, and to have matters settled between us, once
and for all. I awaited his return from the hunt next
day. As the party came through the gates one of the
huntsmen espied me and pointed me out to him. I had
no intention of making an attack, although such was
imputed to me. Can you believe it? The hounds were
hallooed on to me, and I barely escaped by running
swiftly up a tree.

"That night the doors of the castle and of the lodges
were closed against me, and unruly hounds were set
loose. This may have been the doing of the servants
who always disliked me. I went to the castle but not to
bring any protest. I found myself being chased by the
hounds. I crossed one of the walls and betook myself to
Paris. I should, of course, have been delighted to have
had the opportunity of meeting and conversing with
Monsieur Voltaire, but I am sure, Monsieur, that you
will do me the same sort of justice that he would have
done me."

My visitor stayed the night and departed after he
had taken breakfast with me. I fully intended to publish
the history that he related to me. But I saw the Marquise of Carabas at the opera the night after, and I

could not bring myself to publish something that would reflect unfavourably on so adorable a creature. What beauty, what amiability, what radiant charm!

And so I am leaving this with the papers that are to be published posthumously.

THE APPLE

FOR me there is another apple besides the two or three that have glowed in the world's great stories. It rolled upon the floor of an Italic farm-house, and a shrinking maiden looked upon it. And the poet who might have made her name a long-remembered one, made of this maiden's agitation only a figure for his poem.

The apple and the maiden are in Catullus. "As the apple, the lover's whispered gift, slips from the maiden's lap, she forgetting she had hidden it in the folds of her gown; at her mother's entrance she starts to her feet, the apple shaken from its hiding place rolls on the ground, and a guilty blush suffuses her frightened countenance."

And so Catullus leaves the maiden, not aware that he was leaving her in dread suspense for longer than his Rome endured.

I have called the maiden Marcia. Her father voted for old Cato.

Never a wreath had Marcia worn; never had she decked herself with a flower. She laughed seldom and she spoke seldom. She was one of those children whom, when we see them first, we look in the eyes to see if there is not some blindness there. Nevertheless, the sculptor would have praised the grace and vigour of her young body—a body made for endurance and a short summer of beauty.

Yesterday, as she watched the poultry, a fox, heedless of any danger, sprang amongst them. The white cock he would assuredly have carried off. Then Marcia would have had bitter chidings from her stern mother.

But a youth had dashed to the rescue, and the bold fox was made scamper away.

The maiden was left to think on what a youth he was —how much taller and kinder than her brothers. And instead of thinking on the ripening olives and the growing kid, instead of thinking on the clothes she had to wash for her brothers, all her thoughts stayed about the youth, as, in a household, all gather around the hearth.

And he had given an apple to her. With other youths who came to other maidens, he had come to her at the fountain. There he had given her the apple. She had placed it in the soft folds of her gown. As she went back to the house, the savour, the smell, the redness of the apple were all that was for her in thought and vision.

She had sat by the hearth, but at her mother's entrance she started up, and the apple, slipping from the folds of her gown, rolled upon the floor.

The mother took up her spindle, and, standing at one side of the hearth, began to turn the threads. The severe mother! Soon she will look around and see Marcia without a task to her hands.

And the maiden, awakened now from the blankness that was half her life, prays, "Fortune, O Fortune,

The Apple

may my mother not see the apple that Marius gave me!
If she sees it, what shall I say to her? If she looks at
me what will she think about the blush that reddens my
face?"

Silently the mother turns the spindle. A shadow
rests upon the floor, and the shining apple for a while
may not be seen.

Then the mother lays her spindle down. She sits.
When the maiden steals a glance towards her she sees
that she is sleeping.

Fortune, O Fortune!

Marcia takes up the apple. Fair it is, a keepsake and
a talisman! She takes the apple, and once more she hides
it in the soft folds of her gown.